WHAT HAPPENED TO FRANCE

WHAT HAPPENED TO FRANCE

By

GORDON WATERFIELD

*of Reuter's staff and War Correspondent with the
French Armies*

WITH A MAP

LONDON
JOHN MURRAY, ALBEMARLE STREET, W.

First Edition . . . 1940

Made and Printed in Great Britain by Butler & Tanner Ltd., Frome and London

CONTENTS

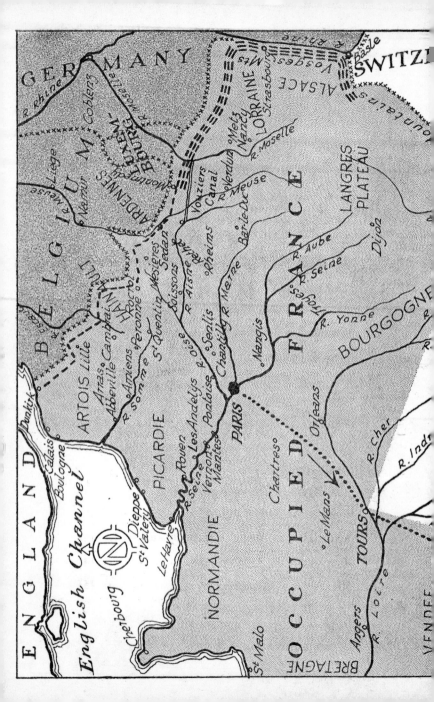

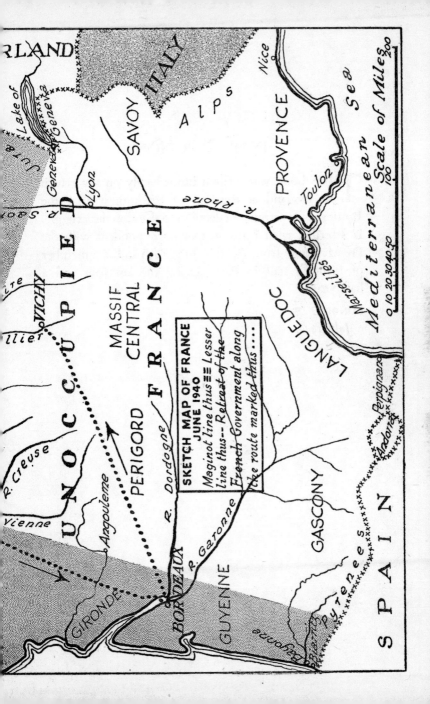

SKETCH MAP OF FRANCE
JUNE 1940
Maginot line thus≡≡ Lesser
line thus— Retreat of the
French Government along
the route marked thus ·····

INTRODUCTION

THIS book was written immediately on my return to England at the end of last month after the Bordeaux Government's decision to abandon the struggle. It describes what I saw as war correspondent with the French armies from April to June 1940 and as a member of Reuter's staff in Paris during the last four and a half years.

LONDON.
July 1940.

CHAPTER I

THE FRENCH TRAGEDY

THE tragic defeat of France will be far-reaching in its effect. Europe, from the Arctic to the Pyrenees, is dominated by Germany, and a hostile Italy stretches across the Mediterranean.

A great nation, whose civilization has permeated the world, has abandoned her independence, and runs the danger of losing herself in Hitler's stranglehold. The balance of power in Europe has been upset and England, with the British Empire, is more gravely threatened than when Napoleon dominated the Continent.

Never has there been so rapid a defeat of a great nation. It all happened in four weeks. On May 15 the German divisions broke through into France on the Meuse and on June 14 they entered Paris. From that moment defeat was almost certain and on June 22 the Armistice was signed at Compiègne.

How did it happen? There were many factors: firstly, for many years France has not been a united nor a well-organized nation ; political and class divisions have weakened the country and prevented parliamentary government from functioning adequately. Secondly, French finance never recovered from the effects of the last war, for she drew too much credit on mythical

German reparation.   Thirdly, the French General Staff
failed to adapt itself to the new mechanized war
which the Germans had tried out in Spain and Poland.
It concentrated too much on defence, suffering from
what has been called " Maginitis," or too great a
belief in the impregnability of the Maginot Line, which
deprived the army of its mobility.   Fourthly, it is a
French characteristic to rely on improvisation ; in the
last war they had time to improvise but in this war
they were rushed off their feet.   No second defence
line was organized to meet the eventuality of the Germans
breaking through the Maginot Line.   All the eggs were
put in one basket.   Once that line was broken the
General Staff and the Government lost hope because
they had not planned to deal with a war of mobility.
Once they had envisaged defeat, as I believe Weygand
did after the break-through on the Meuse, defeat became
probable.   The memories of 1870 defeats became more
insistent than of 1918 victories.   Then began the exodus,
the *sauve qui peut* among the rich, which spread eventually to everyone, as the Germans advanced.   Fifthly, the
French were too civilized to adopt the ruthless methods
of the Germans.   Instead of forcing refugees and soldiers
to stand their ground by shooting them down if necessary, they allowed them to overwhelm France like a
scourge of locusts, blocking lines of communications and
interfering with military operations.   But even if I went
on adding to the list of reasons, as I see them, for the
defeat, it is still very hard to understand.   France has
been beaten in a way that Republican Spain was not

beaten, nor Finland, Poland, Norway nor China. They appear to have lost heart and accepted the conqueror in a way that these others have not.

I believe that the people of France, the patriots among the peasants, the artisans, the mechanics, the shopkeepers, the middle class, the aristocrats and all the rest of them, have not lost heart. If they had been associated more in the councils of the Government through parliament ; if they had been allowed to understand the gravity of the situation before it was too late ; if an appeal had been made to civilians to stand firm in every village of France even if the Germans arrived, and do what they could to sabotage the advance ; if they had defended the houses in their villages and the streets and hills of Paris, there would have been such battles as would have won the admiration of the world and which might have held up the German advance long enough to enable the Allied forces to rally and regroup, it might even have brought America in to turn the scale for the second time in half a century. The French went down with their hands tied behind their backs. They were all mobilized and had to obey the orders of an incompetent general staff and of a government which became a " peace at any price " government. They were badly led, but given a chance they could have been their own leaders, the very thing which the Pétains and the Weygands feared and did their best to prevent. They have not lost heart, but they are now expressionless beneath the heel of the conqueror.

CHAPTER II

THE CULT OF INDIVIDUALISM

FRENCHMEN have a world-wide reputation for clear thinking, but for many years they have been suffering from a confusion in their political philosophy. There has been divided allegiance between *Étatisme* or state control, which worked well under Napoleon Bonaparte but degenerated later into red-tape administration, and individualism, which found its expression in 1789 and subsequent revolutions. The Napoleonic system of administration, with its local prefects under the control of the central government, worked well while the spirit of national efficiency, which had produced the system, survived; but when it had vanished France was left with forty million individualists, each eager to escape from the central control and proud if he succeeded. Frenchmen were delighted if they could score off the administration by avoiding the laws, and every kind of ingenious device was adopted to avoid paying taxes. There were professional advisers in law-breaking who, for a small fee, enabled taxpayers to save thousands of francs a year. Law-makers fell into disrepute because of the number of decrees published, sometimes at variance with those already in force. After having read the many pages of the *Journal Officiel* almost every day for the last few years I am not surprised at the attitude to law adopted by the average Frenchman.

The advent of war increased the number of decrees without very much changing the citizen's point of view. I dined at a well-known Paris restaurant in May this year with a number of foreign journalists, including the correspondent of Stefani, the official Italian news agency, who was my neighbour. It was a day when no restaurant was allowed by law to serve alcohol, as economies were necessary for war purposes. But we had had gin cocktails before dinner and brandy afterwards. The Stefani correspondent was puzzled. I told him that the proprietor of the restaurant had been more than willing to serve us with alcohol, remarking that he considered it was no good having a law unless you broke it every now and again. The Italian was shocked at such indiscipline. At the time I considered that this was merely Fascist priggishness ; but on second thoughts I wondered whether a nation could afford the attractive luxury of indiscipline during a war, when the adversary, Germany, and a potential adversary, Italy, were so well disciplined. For years Germans and Italians, especially the former, have been accustomed to give up their pleasures, while Britain and France continued to live normal lives. Allied propaganda for long insisted that the German people's resisting powers were being weakened by privations. It was seldom suggested that the good-living of the democratic countries might weaken resistance. It takes some time to grow accustomed to the rigid sacrifice which is required in modern

warfare. Even during the " phoney " war period from
September to May, the wealthy French continued to
live in much the same way as before. When the war
came to the gates of Paris, the French feeling for property
prevailed over their desire to win. They had not had
the training that Germans and Italians had had. Pros-
perity had undermined their capacity for taking risks.
They wanted to save their property, save the buildings
of Paris that were dear to them, save the beauty of
France, a beauty which they did not appear to consider
meaningless once it was overrun by the Germans. They
did not stop to think that if and when the time comes
for Paris to be retaken the Germans are not likely to
surrender it without fighting desperately from house to
house, in the same way as they would have defended
Berlin if the Allies had laid siege to it.

The Germans bombed villages, refugees and lines of
communications but they seldom bombed big industrial
plant, which they could easily have done. This may
have been because they wanted to use the plant for
armaments manufacture against England once France
had been defeated. They may also have realized that
the big industrialists would use their influence in favour
of coming to terms when the French armies began to
suffer defeat, hoping that they would have some say in
the management of their factories and be able to continue to draw some of the profits, even if they fell into
German hands. I do not believe that disorganization
was the only reason for the failure to blow up much of
the industrial plant ahead of the German advance.

When the Germans invaded Poland why did not Allied airmen bomb Berlin and the principal towns of Germany? Because they were afraid of reprisals on Paris and London; they dropped leaflets instead. Both Governments maintained their peace-time mentality even when a totalitarian war had been launched. Britain and France kept their peace-time premiers, and the Allies had a peace-time general, Gamelin, as Commander-in-Chief. When Poland was defeated and Germany was free to turn her attention on France, Gamelin withdrew his forces from the Warndt Forest, where they had dominated the industrial region of Saarbrücken and the roads leading to it, because, as he announced at the time, he wanted to save lives. That Gamelin should have thought in those terms was discouraging, since the Allies were fighting a ruthless enemy who did not care how many lives he lost; that he said it publicly had an ill effect on individual soldiers and officers of the French armies. Not only did the French retire from Saarbrücken but they allowed the Germans to take the industrially important French town of Forbach, a few miles to the south-west. This was never announced to the French public. It was only when I visited the front line some months later, in May, and the colonel pointed out the dead chimney stacks of Forbach below, that I realized it was in German hands.

It is true that the war in the west had not yet begun and that the policy was to retire behind the Maginot Line. Any criticism of French inertia was always met by the reply : " France always rises to the occasion in a crisis. Wait until Germany tries to invade France. You will see what will happen." When my Fascist neighbour at the dinner-party I have referred to began talking about the decadence of France, I in my turn used that well-known slogan about France rising to occasions. "That," he replied, "is in itself a form of decadence. A virile people does not wait for a crisis before uniting in national effort. But the French need the most violent shocks in order to react at all. They are supposed to be an intelligent people with quick emotional reaction, and yet the most popular novels and plays are about some abnormal relation like incest, not to mention the vogue that the Grand Guignol has had. The French bourgeoisie is selfish, self-centred and property proud ; he has not been taught to make sacrifices for his country as the Italian bourgeoisie has been taught."

At the time I was angry at such an argument. I felt convinced that the French would acquit themselves well in an emergency. But I thought of the Italian Fascist's conversation as I was dining at this same restaurant two months later when the Germans were little more than twenty miles from Paris. The French Government had abandoned its intention of defending Paris. Reynaud's policy was overridden. The hour had struck for France, but the sense of property was still too strong. They had not rallied. The idea that the Louvre, the Place Vendôme, the Madeleine, their favourite cafés on the Champs Elysées and their houses looking over the Bois de Boulogne might be destroyed helped to make them decide to declare Paris an open town. But there was another factor which weighed with the aged, die-hard Pétain and the religious, reactionary Weygand. Paris was to them a city of revolution. They had a Communist bee in their bonnet and were afraid to call upon the people to help to defend their own capital, fearing that there would be revolution and power would pass into the hands of the extremists of the Left. The story is told on good authority that in Tours, on June 13, General Weygand argued at a meeting of the Government that Communism was rampant in Paris and said that Thorez, leader of the Communist party, which was dissolved last September, had already succeeded in seizing the Elysée. Georges Mandel, the Minister of the Interior, who was in constant touch by telephone with M. Langeron, Prefect of Police, at once exposed this extraordinary story. I was still in Paris on that date with other journalists and there was no sign of any trouble whatever.

CHAPTER III

A NATION DIVIDED AGAINST ITSELF

THE reasons why the Pétains and the Weygands were afraid to call upon the people goes back a long way in French history. The French Revolution lit fires of hatred which have smouldered ever since, being revived periodically, 1830, 1848, 1870 and 1936.

On February 6, 1934, there was an attempt to impose Fascism on France by French big business interests, possibly in agreement with foreign Fascism. The attempt failed and the reply by the people of France came at the general elections, two years later, when the Popular Front (a fusion of the Radical Socialist, Socialist and Communist parties) was returned with a large majority and a Socialist government under Léon Blum came to power. The Blum experiment with its programme of big-scale social reforms was much needed, but it came at a difficult moment for France. French finances were already in a weak state and the new programme was expensive. This could have been dealt with if the country had had time to settle down to the new conditions of this social revolution ; but with the prospect of Blum's advent to power labour tried to press through big demands too quickly and there were strikes which paralysed industry for some time throughout the country.

Blum also made a bad error in introducing the forty-hour week at a time when France needed to produce to the utmost in order to be able to deal with the German menace and provocation from Italy. The bitter feelings between big business on one side and the working classes on the other grew, and at times it seemed almost possible that there might be civil war. Germany and Italy exploited the situation and pressed forward their expansionist programmes before France should have time to settle down to normal life again, while the Soviet government did active propaganda among the Communists and working classes. Internal unrest and the drain of gold from the country, as the wealthy exported their capital, made Blum's position very weak in spite of his big parliamentary majority. It was difficult in these circumstances for France to pursue a firm foreign policy and she became more and more dependent upon Britain.

The animosities aroused between Left and Right in politics were disastrous, and the country's parliamentary life became unstable as politicians grouped and regrouped themselves, trying to manœuvre the majority towards the Left or towards the Right. Prominent men insulted each other in public; people came to blows in cafés, and even at French women's afternoon parties feelings were liable to rise to fever heat. In the timid breasts of industrialists, bankers, clericals and civil servants the old fear of the populace was once more aroused. Divisions and hatreds went so deep that at Bordeaux in the last days of France's independence, just before the Armistice terms with Germany had been accepted, people were saying " better Hitler than Blum." Up to the last there were men like Weygand who feared above everything a popular rising organized by Communists. Rather than that, they were prepared to accept the German terms. Even when France was on the point of being defeated the police were still actively rounding up Communists and Communist sympathizers, whereas for the last year there had been little attempt to round up pro-Fascist sympathizers who were undermining morale even more effectively than the Communists.

Blum eventually was forced out of office largely because of the Senate's hostility, and power shifted to the Radical Socialist party which broke with the Popular Front. Their President was Edouard Daladier, who became Prime Minister. If he had been a strong man he might have formed a national government which would have united the country in time. But he was only the empty shell of a Napoleon. It was said of him that he had the head of a bull but the eyes of a cow. Daladier became Minister of National Defence and the servant of the French Military Staff. He completely identified himself with the views of the Army chiefs at a time when clear-sighted men like Reynaud and Colonel de Gaulle, as he then was, were arguing that the army was failing to adapt itself to the new conditions introduced by Hitler and the German Army chiefs. But whatever doubts the French public may have had when they were told of the big mechanized divisions being formed by the Germans they were always reassured by the magic words : " Maginot Line."

CHAPTER IV

THE MAGINOT LINE THEORY

THE existence of the Maginot Line encouraged France to follow a negative policy in diplomacy and military strategy, which was disastrous in face of Hitler's energy and ambitions. The first indications that France had decided to adopt a " wait and see " policy behind the Maginot Line was given in March 1936 when the Germans marched into the Rhineland and France remained inactive, apart from mobilizing large numbers of fortress troops.

From that moment it became clear to France's allies, Czechoslovakia, Yugoslavia and Poland, that little hope of support could be expected in the event of a sudden attack by Hitler. Germany built the Siegfried Line and France was cut off from sending effective aid to her allies in Europe. She had ceased to be a first-class power. The Quai d'Orsay and the Government realized very well what it would mean to have Hitler occupying the demilitarized zone. Why did not France react more vigorously ? Hitler as usual had chosen his moment for action very well. The general elections were to be held two months later. Albert Sarraut was head of the interim government, and Flandin was Minister of Foreign Affairs. When they found that the British Government

was not prepared to promise any help, they decided not
to make any move. From that moment Hitler never
looked back. If France had been independent enough
to act alone, she could almost certainly have held up the
German divisions and checkmated Hitler's expansionist
policy. Britain would in the end have had to support
her action. But France was not prepared to take any
risks. From that moment the isolationists in France,
such men as Bonnet, Flandin, Laval and the rest, began
to grow in influence, and to intrigue behind the Popular
Front government, which came to office in June 1936.
France had withdrawn behind the Maginot Line, like an
aged tortoise into its shell. Germany was left free to
manœuvre in the rest of Europe ; Yugoslavia was
courted by Italy ; Czechoslovakia and then Poland fell
to Germany. Finally, Germany chose the right moment
to strike at France herself, and she went in like wire
through cheese. The Maginot Line and what it stood
for had sapped France's spirit. She was over-confident
that no one could break through, even though in defer-
ence to Belgium's wishes the Line had not been continued north from Longwy and Montmédy to the sea,
behind Luxemburg and Belgium. Even during those
eight months of waiting, very little was done to
strengthen that weak line of defence. The Germans, on
the other hand, were preparing in every detail an attack
at the weakest part.

When I visited the front line defences as war correspondent during those quiet months before May 10, I
found all the commanding officers eager to show off their

defence works. On the Rhine, north of Strasbourg, an enthusiastic colonel took me from one concrete emplacement to another; day and night soldiers were feverishly working.

"Fine concrete," he kept on muttering as we strode through the woods along the Rhine bank; "they'll never get through this! Magnificent concrete!"

I asked if the Germans had such good concrete on the other side of the Rhine, a few hundred yards away.

"Oh, no," said the colonel, rather coldly, "nothing like so good."

"Is there any reason," I asked, "why you should not attack to prevent them making their defences stronger?"

The colonel smiled reprovingly at me as if I had made a blasphemous remark, but he was too broadminded to take offence at it. He made no reply. The truth was that nobody wanted to attack; their job was to go on making concrete until the Germans took the initiative. On both sides of the Rhine they were building hard, often in full view of each other, but the Germans did not fire on the French, nor the French on the Germans. Every evening a few salvoes were exchanged to relieve the infinite boredom. I spent a night at a well-defended outpost on the banks of the Rhine, and in the morning I walked along the trenches to the look-out post on the water's edge. Across the river a young German was standing in the sun, naked to the waist, washing himself. It annoyed me that it should be possible for him to go on washing calmly there with two machine-guns on the

opposite bank. I asked the French sentry why he did not
fire. He seemed surprised at my bloodthirstiness.

" *Ils ne sont pas méchants,*" he said ; " and if we fire
they will fire back."

The idea that the Germans were not *méchants* was new
to me, and coming from a French soldier was rather surprising. I wondered what effect this constant watching
had on the average French soldier ; seeing the Germans
washing in the morning, and listening to them playing
a concertina in the evening, while others sang sentimental
German songs. It was their business to follow the lives
of the Germans hour by hour and day by day, making
reports. When the concertina ceased to play or the
little white dog was no longer seen running up and down
the bank, they knew that the post had been relieved,
and they began to study the characteristics of the new
occupants through the telescope in the observation post.
It seemed to me that a queer intimacy was likely to spring
up between the watchers on either side. In the mornings
the French used to wake up to see big streamers across
the front of the German outpost, saying : " We don't
want to fight you." " Where are the English ? " or
" The English are with your wives at home." During
the day there were loud-speakers with similar propaganda. The official view was that the propaganda was
so crude and ridiculous that it had no effect, but I wondered if it was so ineffective when I saw what dull lives
the soldiers led on the front line away from their families.
It must have seemed a futile sort of war to some of them
at any rate, and this " why are we fighting ? " propaganda

may have had an effect. I asked a colonel whether he replied to this propaganda.

"No," he said : "war is a serious business to us ; we don't do silly propaganda like that."

But this was a new kind of war, and this middle-aged reserve officer was thinking in terms of 1914. Even if the propaganda had little effect on the German side, it might have had its effect on the French side. A little repartee might have relieved the tedium of those endless days digging defences by the Rhine and living in case-mates, where you could stand upright only in one or two places, and which by June were beginning to ship water from the rising Rhine. Why should the enemy always have the last word ?

The same "friendliness" was to be found on the Maginot Line itself as late as the beginning of June. I visited a fort near Longwy, a little to the south-east of Montmédy, which is the northern end of the Maginot Line proper. Beyond were the small defences—behind the Belgian frontier—which the Germans had broken through in May. They had tried to break through near Montmédy, but hundreds had been killed by the French guns. Our fort jutted like a headland into enemy terri-tory. I was taken on to the sun-baked ridge looking down on the German lines. French soldiers were laying barbed wire entanglements across the ridge in full view of the enemy.

"Don't they fire ?" I asked. I could not resist the usual question though I knew what the answer would be. But after the break-through on May 15 and the invasion of Northern France I had not expected such tranquillity.

"They are working over there and we don't fire on them if they leave us alone," said the young captain with us.

We sat on the ridge watching the puffs of smoke over the German outposts as the French guns made their range-finding tests.

"They are getting ready to fire to-night," said the captain ; "the Germans have already done their range-finding."

I noticed that all the houses of the village where the Germans were, less than a quarter of a mile away, stood intact, but I decided not to ask any more unpopular questions. We left the hot sun and went down into the Maginot Line. It was like going down into a coal-mine. A lift took us into the bowels of the earth, and we walked for a mile along a tunnel, meeting occasional soldiers on bicycles or an electric train bringing up ammunition along a small line. The troops ate, slept and worked underground, seldom going out in the open air. It was like living permanently in the Bakerloo tube. Those who were taken out of the Maginot Line to fill gaps elsewhere must have felt very exposed.

As I drank Pernod in the officers' mess, also underground, I said : "It certainly seems impregnable."

"It's impregnable all right," they said.

All the same there was one form of attack they were nervous about, and that was an attack by parachutists. A single courageous man could put the guns out of action

by throwing incendiary grenades at the gun turrets ; the
heat fuses the metal dome, thus sealing the gun in its
chamber. The officers told me that the Germans had
put the Liège fort guns out of action in this way, and that
they were keeping a sharp lookout to prevent similar
attacks. That was why they were now putting up
barbed wire on the brow of the hill above the fort. If
anyone had suggested to the French military staff some
months before that a few resolute Germans, dropped
from the sky or infiltrating through under cover of night,
could put the guns of the Maginot Line out of action, he
would have been ridiculed or arrested as a defeatist.

It was June 1 when I visited these confident young
men, and on June 14, the same day as the Germans
entered Paris, the Germans broke through the Maginot
Line itself. The German High Command report, which
is generally accurate, states :

In heavy fighting lasting two days against very strong
defence works the Army of General von Witzleben, supported by effective heavy artillery, broke through the
Maginot Line, France's protective wall which was supposed
to be impregnable. They thus broke in two the enemy's
north-eastern front already threatened from the rear, and
shattered the last hopes of the enemy of continuing the
struggle. The French eastern front suffered the same fate
when on June 15 the army commanded by Artillery General
Dollmann overcame near Colmar the powerful defence works
of the Upper Rhine and advanced towards the Vosges. The
Air Force played a big part in the swift breaking through of
the Maginot Line south of Saarbrücken and later near Colmar
and Muelhausen. Whenever weather permitted, dive-

bombers and fighting formations attacked the fortifications with very heavy bombs and silenced their weapons.

And so ended one of the legends of recent years, the impregnability of the Maginot Line. The simple faith placed by the French General Staff in this line of fortifications is one of the tragedies of 1940 and has led to the defeat of France.

CHAPTER V

THE FRENCH GENERAL STAFF

THE French General Staff no longer believed in the Foch principle of the last war that the best defence was in attack. They were haunted by France's low birth-rate and the discrepancy in numbers, 80,000,000 Germans against 40,000,000 Frenchmen. They wished to save their men and they were waiting for the Germans to break their strength in front of the powerful guns of the Maginot Line. They believed that the final issue would be a series of infantry battles and that the French soldier was better than the German. They regarded the tank and the aeroplane as side issues, despite the publicity Germany had given to her own activities in this type of warfare and the experiments made in Spain and Poland. The campaign carried on by Reynaud and de Gaulle in favour of mass production of tanks and 'planes was met with coldness. Several years ago de Gaulle wrote : "To-morrow entire armies will be transported on caterpillars . . . A large fighting unit, striking camp at dawn, will be fifty leagues away by nightfall . . . At least 2,000 tanks will be thrown into the battle." He gives in his book a very accurate description of the methods used by the Germans to break through on the Meuse and on the Somme.

When the French advanced into the Warndt Forest at the beginning of the war, their tanks had considerable success against the German tanks, which were less well protected. Hitler was quick to realize the importance of speeding up production, and during the following eight months an enormous number of tanks were built, so that in June, according to the French military authorities, he was able to throw 4,000 tanks into the final battle for France.

Even over the question of defence the French General Staff was not thorough. The Maginot Line proper covered only half the French frontier, from Basle to Montmédy and Longwy, where the Belgian frontier begins. It was never constructed northwards to the sea behind the Belgian frontier, and it is very misleading that every British war map that I have seen represents the Maginot Line as continuous from the North Sea to the Swiss frontier. The French had intended to continue the line of strong fortifications northwards, but the Belgian Government had stated that they would consider it an unfriendly act, so that only a weak line was built. The French relied instead on the Dutch and Belgians resisting invasion long enough to enable British and French reinforcements to arrive, a plan which saved them the expense of building a new line at a time when their finances were not very strong.

It was clearly mistaken economy, for if and when the German attack came it was almost certain to be on the weakest part of the line behind Belgium. There was nothing new in the German plan of attack. It was the old von Schlieffen plan of 1913, with a strong right wing pivoting on the left. Once the break-through had been effected north of Sedan, and the French armies were in retreat, the German armies pivoted on their left wing near Sedan, a little north of the end of the Maginot Line at Montmédy and Longwy. They made sure of separating the British, Belgian and French armies from the main body of the French armies by pushing towards the Channel ports ; once that manœuvre was successfully carried out, they resumed the classic plan and swung south towards the Seine.

The French General Staff should have known that Hitler would try to break through in the region of the Meuse, for it was one of the weakest points in the French defences. De Gaulle wrote in his book several years ago :

It is true that the heights of the Moselle and those of the Meuse, abutting at one end on the Lorraine plateau and at the other on the Ardennes, offer considerable obstacles, but they have no depth, and a single error, sudden surprise or momentary negligence would suffice for their loss, rendering vulnerable from the rear any movement of withdrawal in Hainault or Flanders. It so happens that in those low plains there is neither wall nor dyke on which the line of resistance can anchor itself ; no line of dominating heights, no rivers running parallel to the front. Worse still, the lie of the land favours invasion by reason of the many routes of penetration, such as the valleys of the Meuse, the Sambre, the Scarpe and the Lys, where rivers, highroads and railways offer themselves as guides to the enemy.

It was precisely this point that the Germans attacked,

following the Meuse southwards through Holland and
Belgium, past Maastricht, Liège and Namur to Rocroi,
Mezières and Sedan in France. The two armies holding
this part of the French Meuse were the Ninth Army under
General Corap, and, on his right flank in the Sedan
sector, the Second Army under General Huntziger.
The Corap army was not a strong army. General Corap
had repeatedly begged headquarters for more material
to build defences and better arms for his troops. Whenever he was visited by war correspondents, he had always
the same story to tell—lack of supplies. Corap was made
the scapegoat when the German armoured divisions
broke through into France, but the responsibility was
with the General Staff, as was, I believe, shown in the
investigation carried out after the break-through. There
is indirect criticism of the General Staff in Reynaud's
striking *La Patrie est en danger* speech to the Senate. He
said : " The Meuse, apparently a difficult river to cross,
had been wrongly considered as a redoubtable obstacle
for the enemy. That is the reason why the French
divisions which were entrusted with its defence were few
and were spread out over a great area along the river.
In addition, the army of General Corap, which was composed of divisions not so well officered and less well
trained, was put there, the best troops forming part of
the left wing marching into Belgium.

" The Meuse is a difficult river and difficult to defend.
Machine-gun fire on the flank is impossible and infiltration is easy for manœuvring troops. We can add to that
the fact that more than half the infantry divisions of the

Corap army had not yet reached the Meuse, although
they had the shortest movement to make.   That was not
all.   As a result of incredible mistakes, which will be
punished, the bridges over the Meuse were not destroyed.   Over these bridges there passed the German
armoured divisions, preceded by fighter 'planes which
came to attack divisions which were scattered, ill-cadred
and badly trained for such attacks.   You can now understand the disaster and the total disorganization of the
Corap army.

" It was thus that the pivot of the French Army was
broken. . . .   A breach of about 60 miles wide had been
opened in our front.   Into this breach poured a German
army composed of motorized divisions, which, after
having caused a large bulge in the direction of Paris,
turned west, towards the sea, taking in the rear our entire
fortified system along the Franco-Belgian frontier and
threatening the Allied forces still engaged in Belgium, to
whom the order to retreat was not given until the evening of May 15."

" The Meuse," said Reynaud, " had wrongly been
considered as a redoubtable obstacle for the enemy. . . .
It is difficult to defend, machine-gun fire on the flank is
impossible and infiltration is easy for manœuvring
troops."   De Gaulle had said this in his book ; every
Army officer who studied topography knew it.   Yet the
General Staff placed there what they knew to be a weak
army.   The arrest and perhaps the shooting of generals
and other commanding officers does not take away
responsibility from Gamelin and the General Staff.

Their plan was to help defend the Belgian frontier and to make that their front line.   But they had long known that the Belgian temper was uncertain and that Leopold was not entirely to be counted on as a friend of France.

CHAPTER VI

INVASION OF THE WEST

ON the night of Thursday and Friday, May 9/10, the Germans invaded Holland. The methods they used were extraordinary and sometimes ingenious, and the stories brought to France by Belgian and Dutch refugees about parachutists helped to spread suspicion and confusion almost as disorganizing as the presence of the parachutists themselves.

These were some of the devices which caused disorganization. At dawn on Friday the Germans landed about fifty soldiers in Dutch uniform by seaplane on the river in Rotterdam; they landed in rubber boats and captured the bridges, but were eventually all killed or taken prisoner. In The Hague Germans got into the city dressed as Dutch soldiers and began firing from the roofs. Dutch soldiers then went up to the roofs and were taken for Germans and killed by their compatriots. A few of the Boy Scouts who were responsible for the A.R.P. work were Germans, and began firing at the Dutch soldiers, with the result that all the Boy Scouts fell under suspicion and A.R.P. work was held up. A story went round, probably spread by fifth columnists, that there was a German car running round the streets throwing gas grenades. It was never established whether or not this was true, but everyone began looking for the car. Soldiers belonging to the Palace Guard died from smoking poisoned cigarettes. German housemaids who had been recalled to their country some months previously were brought back into Holland with baskets of provisions which concealed hand grenades for fifth columnists and German soldiers. No one knew who was friend and who was foe.

There were three types of parachutists : firstly, the well-trained soldiers who had detailed maps of places where they landed and full information about where soldiers were billeted and what regiments they belonged to. They had addresses of Nazi sympathizers and among the orders found on these men there was always the phrase : " Let everyone pass who has a certificate with a photograph signed by the German Chief of Police." Secondly, there were young fanatical Nazis with a lust to kill. They shot at everything they saw, women, children, sheep, etc. ; when they had finished their ammunition some were seen to burst into tears. One boy came down dressed as a Red Cross nurse and was found to be in possession of several hand grenades. Thirdly, there were young parachutists dropped in bunches who were usually frightened, and gave themselves up as soon as they had landed.

While confusion was being created in this way the Germans landed a whole division, about 17,000 men, by troop-carrier 'planes. Parachutists, followed by troops in old 'planes, captured aerodromes, which were subsequently taken back, and a good many troops were landed by 'plane on the beach at Schevening. Some of them came across the frontier in armoured cars painted with the Dutch colours. The most effective betrayal was the capture of the Moerdyk bridge across the Hollandsch Diep. It was well defended as it was an extremely important line of communication into the heart of Holland. Somehow the Germans were landed on the south side of the bridge dressed in Dutch uniform and in Dutch cars. They managed to persuade the garrison of the bridge that they brought orders from Dutch headquarters that they should withdraw to a point farther south. The whole garrison left without firing a shot and the Germans took possession of the bridge. When headquarters learnt of this they ordered the garrison of 200 to go straight back and recapture the bridge ; all were killed trying to rush the guns of their own fort.

By Saturday a French armoured division had arrived and was asked to retake the bridge, otherwise the road would be open to German mechanized divisions. According to the Dutch High Command it should have been an easy task for a few tanks. General Giraud realized the importance of retaking it, and gave an order accordingly, but for some reason it was never carried out. The bridge was not even blown up. Finally the German armoured divisions arrived and poured over this bridge, into Belgium and on to France. If that bridge could have been held it is possible that the German advance would have been delayed for sufficient time for the Allies to establish themselves behind the Dutch defences. After five days of gallant defence the "cease fire" was ordered on May 14. In Zeeland fighting continued for a few days more.

CHAPTER VII

THE BREAK-THROUGH ON THE MEUSE

TWO other war correspondents, David Scott of *The News Chronicle* and George Miller of *The Daily Express*, and myself were near Sedan, attached to the G.H.Q. of the 2nd Army commanded by General Huntziger, when the Germans broke through on the Meuse. On May 14 we drove from Cambrai to Vouziers and on to G.H.Q. a little farther north. All the last fifty miles of our journey we saw mournful columns of refugees from Holland, Belgium, Luxemburg and from the French frontier region. Among them were old men and women who had already made the 1914 trek; a few even had experienced the 1870 invasion when Napoleon III was defeated at Sedan. Many pushed perambulators and handcarts, others were on bicycles, on ice-cream wagons, even on hearses; cart-horses, which should have been working the fields, were pulling large hay wagons—three or four horses to a wagon—which held as many as fifty women and children with all their cooking utensils, blankets and mattresses. Whole villages had migrated together in a community, and occasionally stopped by the roadside to cook food which became scarce after several days on the road; few had money to buy more. I saw middle-aged women walking down the interminable straight roads for hours and days on end, carrying a suitcase in either hand. The populations of four countries were on the move, slowly, doggedly working south, away from the Germans. It was the beginning of a movement which, being joined by increasing numbers daily, was eventually to block French roads, disorganize food and petrol supplies, and hamper the military engaged on one of the greatest and most critical battles in history.

Those I spoke to who had arrived by car said that the German mechanized divisions were pushing south along the Albert Canal and the Meuse, both of which they had been able to cross as bridges had not been blown up. The refugees had left their houses at a few moments' notice, so quick was the advance. On the way many of them had been bombed and machine-gunned. We knew that refugees were always liable to think that the enemy was hot on their track, so that we were sceptical at first, but it was not long before we found that their stories were in general true.

On the way to headquarters we had to stop quite frequently as German 'planes flew overhead bombing road and railway communications behind the front line. The village headquarters of the 2nd Army seemed very peaceful in comparison to the open road and we were able to take off our steel helmets and take out our typewriters. Captain Massis, head of the Army's press section, made us very comfortable and gave us an office as our press room during the two days we were to be there. He told us that the Germans, having advanced rapidly south through Belgium and Luxemburg, were preparing a big offensive against the French defence line on the Meuse in the Sedan region either for the same evening or the next morning. " You have arrived at a very interesting moment," he said. Massis had been on a tour the last few days across the frontier into Belgium with General Huntziger. He had found the Belgians extraordinarily unprepared for resistance, and the civilian population had not seemed to realize the gravity of the situation. The mayor of Bouillon, a small town in Belgium, had said to him : " We are all right here. This village is only a small tourist centre and the Germans are not likely to do any damage." The next day the village was heavily bombed, probably with the object of getting the civilian population on the move towards the French frontier, so as to embarrass military operations. The captain gave us a description of how the Germans were expected to attack, which turned out to be very accurate. He said that they would use their 'planes like artillery, heavily bombing the front lines and machine-gunning the troops. While the latter were taking cover the Germans would drop parachutists, armed with machine-guns, who would take up defensive positions until they were joined by mechanized columns. Thus he went on, as if giving a conference at the Sorbonne on military strategy, instead of describing a bloody battle that was about to be fought. It was an interesting story for us, and we were assured that our copy would be taken to the headquarters of the military censorship near Paris by special courier and would be in London very rapidly. We sat down to our typewriters and did an " Eve of the Battle " story which was very exciting reading, but unfortunately it did not get to London until the German divisions had broken through and the 2nd and 9th Armies were in retreat. France was to suffer a second Sedan defeat, and again they were to be beaten back to the Loire, but this time there was to be no Gambetta to rally the country.

On May 14, however, Captain Massis and other officers of the G.H.Q. were confident of success. " We are withdrawing our advance posts, as has always been our intention," he said, " but we will hold the Germans on our main defence line." He told us that General Huntziger would like to see us that evening or the next morning and would arrange to take us as near the battle as possible. It turned out, however, that the General was too busy. We learnt that G.H.Q. was going to be moved back that night, and there were rumours of a break-through on our left, where Corap's army was trying to hold an extensive front. Instead of seeing the General we had to be content with reading his Order of the Day to the troops, which he had just issued. It said that they must on no account retreat from their posts on the Maginot Line, defending the sacred soil of France. It was a heroic message from a general to his troops, from a general who six weeks later was to head the armistice delegation to sign the terms of capitulation.

We motored back to Vouziers with our Press Lieutenant, who was disconsolate, having had to cancel his arrangements for a performance by well-known stage personalities, which was to have taken place at Sedan the next day ! We spent the night in Vouziers but there was little sleep. All the time outside my window lorries and tanks were rumbling by, going up to the front line. The whole town was full of refugees sleeping in the streets and public square. Many German agents must have come in with them to communicate French troop movements to the Germans only a few miles away, cut communications and help to spread panic among the civilian population. France, having been so careful to weed out suspicious foreigners during the last few years, was now, at a critical moment, being invaded by a host of men, women and children of various nationalities, who were even passing through the Maginot Line itself. Such an invasion must have been foreseen, but no attempt was made to stop the refugees on the Belgian and Luxemburg frontiers until it was too late. They should have been stopped by rifle fire if necessary and everyone should have been made to stay in the French villages until they could be evacuated in proper order by train and lorries.

The G.H.Q. of the 2nd Army moved during the night and were too busy to bother about us at Vouziers, where we remained to glean a lot of interesting but depressing information from the soldiers who were seeking shelter in the village from the front line. The stragglers came into the cafés in the main square, first in twos and threes and then in groups. The Germans, they said, had broken through the Meuse defences at certain points.

This was very bad news, for it meant that the army would have to fight a mobile war when they had prepared only for a defensive war.   We had no means of checking the soldiers' stories and had to wait patiently in the hope that we would learn what was happening from G.H.Q. All the soldiers complained of the terrible effect of the German dive-bombing over them.   They had not been trained to be accustomed to any such attacks ; the noise of the planes charging down to within a few feet of their heads was, they said, frightening enough, apart from the bombs.   " Where are the French 'planes ? " they kept on saying.   " We saw nothing but German all the time. They played about as if they were at home."   All the soldiers looked tired, bedraggled and dazed.   There was repeated bombing during the morning, the Germans trying to hit the railway and road over the Aisne, which were being used to rush up reinforcements in an attempt to stop the gap.   As I went out of the hotel to buy some cigarettes I looked up and saw two Dorniers flying straight down the street towards me just above the roof-tops, machine-gunning as they came.   The next second I was lying full length down a side street with a lot of other people.   Fortunately they had let go all their bombs.   Some way down the road just outside the town a huge column of black smoke was rising. Scott, Miller and I went to investigate.   A military petrol convoy had been hit and was burning hard. Each side of the road, every two or three hundred yards, there were large bomb craters ; no direct hits had been scored.   The heat was intense near the convoy and every now and again ammunition was exploding. In a field nearby, an officer lay dead, stretched on his back, his eyes staring into the bright sun. In another field a wounded soldier was crying for help : we got the ambulance to him. All along the road were abandoned water bottles and bits of equipment. The German 'planes came back once or twice. Miller and I threw ourselves into the ditch by the side of the road. Scott went off by himself into the fields. He said that he found the placid chewing of the cows was very reassuring during a bombardment.

I went to look for the mayor, as I heard that there were many refugees in the hospital who had been machine-gunned and bombed on the road. I found him in the main square looking very harassed. He had had thousands of refugees through the town every day, and it was a big problem to feed them and to try to find means of transport. He took me to the hospital, where his daughter was working. One after another wounded refugees were being taken to the operating table, which was clearly visible to everyone walking in and out of the hospital. The doctors told me that several of them had been machine-gunned ; the others had been bombed. Did I want to talk to them ?

" No, I didn't want to bother them."

" Oh, it wouldn't bother them at all."

They took me into a big ward full of wounded women and cross-examined these unfortunate people, while I stood uncomfortably in the background. They were mostly French from the Ardennes, and a number of them had definitely been machine-gunned while on the roads. The 'planes had come down low before firing and could see that they were only refugees : there were no French soldiers anywhere near. I was made to talk to a man who had just had his arm amputated at the shoulder. His bed was covered in blood but he spoke coherently. While I was in the ward bombs fell a little distance away and blew open the windows. It was terrible to see the panic among these wounded men, women and children, who tried to get out of bed. The doctors did their best to soothe them and gradually the panic died down. As I went out a man was being carried in who had been injured by one of the bombs which we had heard fall. The doctors' work was almost continuous. If the refugees had only stayed where they were they would probably have been safe, and the doctors would have been free to carry on their proper work of looking after the wounded soldiers, who were beginning to pour into Vouziers from the Meuse battle. There would have been room, too, in the civilian hospitals to take soldiers from the overflowing military hospital. In the street old men and women were repeatedly coming up to ask whether they ought to stay or go ; we always told them to stay where they were, but the urge to get away from the Germans and the repeated bombing was too much for them. They all began to pack up and leave. The hotel where we had dined the evening before was closed down and the people had left. At eleven in the morning I had bought some typewriting paper from the bearded proprietor of the stationer's shop ; he was a typical bourgeois with a hard collar and a black suit, who had owned and lived in the shop for the last twenty years and looked as if he was a fixture there for another twenty ; but by midday he had put on his black hat and he too was on the road, pushing a wheelbarrow with a few household goods and perspiring freely.

In the middle of this confusion we were given a very welcome gin and vermouth at the Mess of the M.T.C. by their commanding officer, Miss Betty Scott. A group of eight British women were at Vouziers attached to the French Army, driving cars for the *Service Sanitaire*, taking captured German airmen to headquarters, and driving wounded refugees to hospital. An example of the fatalistic way in which these people were abandoning their houses was given us by Miss Scott, who said that her landlady had departed the day before and had handed her the keys of her villa. Miss Scott had suggested that she should take them with her, for it was not certain by any means that the Germans would reach Vouziers.

"No," said the woman, "I took the keys away with me in 1914 and when I came back the keys were all I had left. It isn't worth taking them."

It was part of the German strategy, I believe, to get the civilian population on the move. When Rotterdam was bombed, the Germans intended to destroy as much of the town as possible in order to intimidate the Dutch commanding officer, but in France they were using light bombs which could be distributed over a wide area, so that a maximum number of people were affected. This migration of the population played a big part in the six weeks' campaign. I understand that there was at least one bridge across the Meuse which was not blown up because it was crowded with refugees, and the French were not ruthless enough to destroy them with the bridge. Other bridges were left through incompetence or treachery, and in some places the Germans crossed by driving a number of tanks into the river and rushing the other tanks over on top. The advance was rapid and ruthless. The Germans paid no attention to refugees on the road, and even drove the tanks over their own wounded rather than suffer delay.

While the most critical of battles was being fought only twenty-five miles away we were getting restless, for we were deprived of all reliable news, being fed only on what could be gleaned from refugees and straggling soldiery. We were relieved when we saw our rather agitated Press Lieutenant arrive, but he brought very little information apart from the fact that the big battle was proceeding and that things were not going over well. The German mechanized divisions had crossed the Meuse and their tanks and armoured columns were advancing rapidly. I do not believe that the G.H.Q. of the 2nd Army itself had a very clear knowledge of what was happening. They had moved during the night to a château which had only one telephone and it was difficult for them to make contact with anyone at first. The Corap army was breaking up on the left of us and the Germans had broken through the defences behind Belgium, wrongly described as the Maginot Line. We were naturally anxious to know as much as possible and asked to be taken to army headquarters, as had been arranged. But as usual it had been decided that we should be pushed back so that we should see as little as possible of what was happening. The lieutenant seemed to be upset even that we had been talking to stragglers in Vouziers. His orders were that we should be taken to Verdun which was near the new headquarters. Verdun then seemed a long way from the battle but we had to go. There was no question of returning to Cambrai, where we had left all our clothes in the rooms reserved for us by the military authorities, as the Germans were advancing rapidly in that direction. Only two days before we had protested at being sent so far from the front line as Cambrai ! We stayed the night at Verdun and the next morning Captain Massis arrived from G.H.Q. He had been told by the lieutenant that we had been talking with soldiers from the front line at Vouziers and he also was annoyed, taking pains to explain that they were obviously not representative of the French Army. He insisted that we should go back to Paris as quickly as possible but said that he could not have us motored there as all the press cars (there were eight allocated to each army) were needed for other work. We protested strongly at being sent back just at a moment when we could justify our existence as war correspondents, and give accounts to the French and British Press of the gallant fight being put up by the French armies. Instead of only seeing the stragglers we could have seen something of the fighters. But it was no good arguing, and even if we had got news there was no way of getting it out, except through the G.H.Q., for it was impossible to telephone or telegraph outside the department. We agreed, therefore, with a bad grace. Captain Massis sent us to Bar le Duc, where there was supposed to be a train in two hours' time for Paris. When we arrived we found that all trains had been stopped for some days, and there was no car to be hired because they were all requisitioned for refugees who were crowding hourly into the town. We had to wait patiently, and stay there the night. The only excitement was some slight bombing and the temporary arrest of David Scott as a parachutist. Finally, at mid-day next day, the train left, crowded with refugees and soldiers, some of them wounded. Two wounded in our carriage had been turned out of a hospital in Bar le Duc to make room for the few survivors of a regiment which had been nearly wiped out by bombing as it was being convoyed to the front line. The journey took eighteen hours instead of the normal two ! Shortly after passing a derelict train which had been gutted by bomb shrapnel and by fire, the train stopped. There had been an air-raid warning and the 'planes had cut the line a mile in front. A few seconds later we heard the 'planes overhead, and that all too familiar whistle as six bombs fell in the field a hundred yards away in a line parallel to the train. Once more I was surprised to find how quickly and instinctively one fell prone at the whistling of the bombs. I was standing in a crowded corridor, elbow to elbow with French soldiers, and we

all went down together. I must have got there first,
for I found two French soldiers on top of me, which was
a satisfactory protection against bomb shrapnel. The
only trouble was that long after the 'planes had gone
the soldiers were still there and I was beginning to
suffocate. When the first shock was over pandemonium
broke loose. Women and children rushed out of the
train, across the fields to a wood a mile away ; others
crawled under the train and remained there for the next
hour. We tried to calm people down. Miller looked
after a mother and her baby, and I felt almost proud of
my " parachutist " uniform when a small girl took my
hand and said to her mother : " I want to stay with
the officer ! " I went back into our carriage to get one
of the cushions to put over her head in case the 'planes
came back, and found " old soldier " Boursier, the
correspondent of the *Intransigeant*, who had been through
three campaigns, lying full length on the seat with both
cushions on top of him, smoking a cigarette. I removed
one cushion and gave it to the girl and her mother.
Another mother wanted me to find her small boy, who
had run away in a panic. I found him two fields away,
running about aimlessly. " No, no, I can't go back to
that train," he kept on saying. Eventually I picked him
up and carried him back, but a few minutes later he was
off again. Everyone was frightened the 'planes would
come back, which in fact they did, to bomb the station.
Five bombs fell only fifty yards from the engine, and
blew out all the station windows ; the only loss of
life was three chickens, and one rabbit, wounded. No

damage was done to the train and no one was injured. The chief damage was to telephone lines, so that we could not find out how badly destroyed the line ahead had been. After about half an hour the engine blew ten terrific blasts on its whistle to call back the fugitives in the woods, and in another half-hour we were all collected and steaming slowly to the place where the line had been cut. Already the workmen were on the job and in about an hour it was mended. During that hour's wait the crowds were beginning to start parachute hunting. The story went round that a priest had been seen with a suspicious white tin box, but he was not discovered. If Miller, Scott and I had known then what was happening to two of our colleagues, who had been held up at Cambrai, we might have felt more self-conscious about our uniforms than we were already.

A word should be said about our uniforms. If the war correspondents had been formed into a platoon and marched down the Champs Elysées on a Sunday evening it would have been a magnificent entertainment for the crowds along the Boulevards. The individualism which has always been one of the characteristics of the French, found full expression in their uniforms ; added to that, there were the British Correspondents trying to look like English officers, and American Correspondents trying to look like American officers. We had no rank, but decided in committee that we should only salute officers superior to captains. On our shoulder-straps there was a piece of green cloth with the inscription " War Correspondent," which was supposed to explain our identity to a French population. On our hats, forage caps and berets we wore a large gold " C," or " CG," which stood for *Correspondent* or *Correspondent de Guerre*. When War Correspondents first appeared on the streets of Paris, the humorous French weekly, the *Canard Enchainé*, decided that our hat badges stood for " *Cocu* " or " *Cocu Garanti*," and we were described as " moitiés soldats." Our tunics were of different coloured cloth, and of differing cut ; buttons were leather, or general service, or Rifle Brigade, or nondescript. The covering of the lower part of the body was also a matter of taste, and finally there was a surprising diversity of physique. Half of us would not have been accepted by any army in the world, and certainly not to serve as parachutists in the German Army. But the crowd-mind did not reason logically. We were something peculiar, neither soldier nor officer, and therefore we were suspect.

CHAPTER VIII

MASS HYSTERIA

THE adventures of the journalists who went back to Cambrai are worth telling as they show how contagious hysteria can be. These columns of refugees, who plodded on wearily and doggedly for days, would suddenly, owing to German 'planes overhead or some scare story, start a panic which spread rapidly and generally ended up by engulfing the local authorities themselves. Periodically a story would pass along the column like wind across a wheatfield and they would throw themselves on any passing car, troop lorry or ambulance, in a frenzy to get away.

Among the war correspondents left at Cambrai on May 15, were Percy Philip of *The New York Times*, Taylor Henry of the "Associated Press" and Maurice Noel of the *Figaro*. The Army Press Officer had left them in the evening, stating that he would return the next morning to take them on a trip to the front line. But during the night the G.H.Q. in Cambrai learnt that the front was coming unpleasantly close to them and decided to move hastily. The journalists, sleeping peacefully in their beds, were forgotten. They had their coffee the next morning and waited for the Press Officer. By midday they grew restless and went to inquire at the *Place Militaire*, where they were greeted with astonishment by the few officers who had remained there. "Good heavens! What are you doing here?" they said. "Don't you know that the Germans are approaching Cambrai and that G.H.Q. has moved back? You must leave at once by the next train." The three journalists packed their bags and deposited them at the station, which was crowded with refugees who were waiting for a train due to leave in an hour's time. The journalists went to have a drink and were returning half an hour later when German 'planes came over and destroyed a good part of the station. Philip went to see if he could rescue his typewriter and suitcase which he had left in the stationmaster's office. He opened the door: six dead bodies lay by his typewriter, so he left it. The station was so damaged that it was clear there could be no train through it for some days; the majority of the refugees had managed to take cover, but a number of dead lay on the platforms. The three went off to buy bicycles. As they were about to ride out of the town, the 'planes came back. Taylor Henry had no time to get off: the explosion of a bomb carried away his back wheel and he was thrown over the handlebars. The other two escaped with fewer bruises. They waited while Henry went back to the shop and had another wheel put on. Then they started on their ride to Paris. There was a difference in their bicycling capacities, and after the first day they got separated. Philip decided to take a train, while the other two went on separately.

Philip is tall and tough-looking ; he is a Scotsman. In his uniform as a war correspondent he probably conformed as nearly as anyone to the popular conception of a German parachutist. He was in a train that was bombed and the passengers got excited. The newspapers and the French wireless stations had told people to be on the look-out for parachutists, and they were only obeying their instructions when four French soldiers and a captain arrested Philip. Unfortunately they were in such an emotional state that they would not accept any of his official papers as genuine, and they would not take him to the nearest police station. They had made up their minds the first moment they saw him that they were going to shoot him. Philip had lived fourteen years in France, but none of his arguments prevailed. When he pointed out that he had the red ribbon of the Legion of Honour, they were aghast that even a German should have such effrontery ; when he showed them his papers carefully supplied by General Gamelin's headquarters with numerous official stamps, they said that he was clearly suspect because he had too many papers. They made him take off his riding boots and they searched him thoroughly. When they found nothing incriminating, they said : " We are wasting time. Stand over there and we will shoot you." " I will give the *coup de grâce*," shouted the Captain, waving his revolver. The crowd round was in complete agreement, shouting out " *sale Boche !* " Philip had one hope : he knew that the gendarmes had been sent for, and he played for time.

" Surely you will let a Scotsman put on his boots before you shoot him ? "

Grudgingly they consented. He took as long as possible pulling on his high boots and before he was finally dressed several hefty mobile guards arrived. They forced their way through the crowd and marched the prisoner off. They said that his papers were correct but they refused to take any responsibility for his safety.

" The crowd is in such a dangerous mood that we cannot do anything for you," they said. " You must get away as best you can."

He thanked them and managed to win the sympathy of three army doctors who said that they would see that he was all right ; with them he got away from the danger zone while the crowd were busy hunting for other victims.

Noel, the French Correspondent, is also rather Germanic in looks and physique, but he was not conscious of this as he bicycled into a peaceful French village and stopped to have a glass of red wine. He is very deaf and he did not know that the German 'planes had been bombing near the village just before he arrived. Gradually the people began to come out of their cellars and to collect round him. As in the case of Philip, the crowd at once took him to be a German. He tried to drown their accusations by making a long speech at the top of his voice, like Danton trying to control an angry revolutionary mob. Whenever he stopped to draw breath, the women's cry was taken up : " The newspapers have told us to kill all parachutists."

The crowd grew larger as the story went round the village that they had caught a parachutist. Even Noel found slight comic relief in the fact that an Arab soldier from Algeria came up and shook his fist under Noel's nose, shouting : " I can tell by your accent that you are not a Frenchman." By this time the police had heard that a parachutist had been caught and arrived to deal with him. They bustled him off to the police station followed by the crowd. It was a hot day and everyone was excited. The police themselves had caught the general hysteria, and the fat, red-faced sergeant was so carried away that he could not even read Noel's papers.

The police carried out a thorough search while the crowd shouted that he should be killed. Noel had taken off his top boots as it was so hot, and had hung them on the handlebars of the bicycle. In them was found a box of white powder which he took against indigestion.

" There it is," they shouted. " There is the explosive."

" Nonsense ! " he yelled. " I will prove that it isn't explosive."

He lighted a match to make his demonstration, but before he could put the flame to the powder, three police officers, ten men and a number of women had flung themselves on him in a desperate attempt to save the police station from total destruction. A diversion was created by the arrival of the Mayor, who had a lot of influence in the village. He was sensible and courageous. After looking at Noel's papers he realized that everything was in order and that the best way to get him away was to have him handed over to the nearest military authorities.

Perhaps the worst part of the story is to come. When the war correspondents had arrived at Cambrai a few days before, we had been received by a Colonel who was very eager to make us as comfortable as possible, and arranged for us to have a press room, a telephone and an Army stenographer to do the typing. (There were about twenty eminent French journalists and only two of them could use a typewriter.) Noel had subsequently been with him on a visit to one of the armies and had got to know the Colonel quite well. He was therefore very relieved to learn that he was to be taken to this Colonel. Noel by then had been bicycling hard for two days away from the front, and it struck him as curious that the Colonel should have kept up with him, but he did not at the time trouble very much about it. He found the Colonel and greeted him enthusiastically, feeling that at last his identity could be established and his troubles ended. The Colonel, however, was apparently suffering from amnesia ; he said that he did not recognize either Noel or his papers, and had him put under arrest. In the morning, however, Noel was told that he was free to go and he went without seeing the Colonel. The latter was in trouble with his headquarters ; he had been responsible for the journalists at Cambrai and he had left before he had orders to do so.

Similar incidents of crowd panic occurred at some time or another in almost every village and town of

France, disorganizing all the local service such as the fire brigade and first aid. French and British pilots were manhandled and French soldiers nearly lynched. There were, of course, also many instances of real parachutists coming down and being caught. The crowds were right to keep a lookout, as Reynaud stated in his speech to the Senate,

> Our classic conception of the conduct of war has come up against a new conception. At the basis of this conception, there is not only the massive use of heavy armoured divisions or co-operation between them and aeroplanes, but the creation of disorder in the enemy's rear by means of parachute raids. I will not speak to you of the false news and the orders given by means of the telephone to the Civil Authorities, with the object, for example, of causing hurried evacuations. The Senate will understand that of all the tasks which confront us the most important is clear thinking. We must think of the new type of warfare which we are facing and take immediate decisions !
>
> The Government has already taken decisions. You know its first actions. No failure will be tolerated. Death is a very mild punishment for any offence against the vital interests of the country. At a time when our soldiers are dying, there will be no more dilatory procedure with regard to traitors, saboteurs or cowards. There is no longer a place for any vested interest. Let us rise to the misfortunes of the country.

Reynaud made that speech on May 21, a week after the invasion of France. All that time refugees and enemy agents had been allowed to pour into the country. Still no plan to deal with this vast question had been drawn up. Without orders, many of the French local officials, always very dependent upon the central Government, were at a loss to know what to do, and the people tended at moments of crisis to take the law into their own hands, which added to the confusion. Every village and every town wanted to know the answers to such questions as : were they to stop the refugees or send them on ; if the latter, how were they to be sent ? If they were to stay, how were they to be fed ? Were the towns-people and villagers to remain where they were, or were they to be allowed to swell the migrating mass of human beings, and add to the difficulties of the authorities in the next stopping-place farther south or west ? It was clearly a national problem, to be settled by the central Government or by the General Staff. Some of the local authorities, when they found that communications were cut off with Paris as a result of bombing or sabotage, jumped into their cars and left for the capital to try to find out what to do. As a result of the crowded state of the roads, many of them failed to return and their own people were left to fend for themselves. There were a few who departed without any intention of returning, because they knew that the Germans were approaching.

It is easy to be wise after the event, but it is the duty of governments to have foreseen such eventualities as arose in France. Firstly, refugees from Holland, Belgium and Luxemburg should not have been allowed to enter France. Secondly, after May 10, when Holland, Belgium and Luxemburg were invaded, no French person should have been allowed to leave his locality without

special permission.   Thirdly, it should have been pointed
out to citizens that by leaving the countryside and the
villages untenanted they were helping the enemy, since
German agents could carry out their work of sabotage
unwatched and undisturbed.   Besides keeping a lookout
for parachutists, they should have been told to build
barricades and have glass to throw on the roads should
German motor-cyclists and cars approach.

To do all this would have required a high degree of
courage on the part of the French citizen.   But I believe
that if the local authorities had been present to encourage
them and to keep them busy preparing methods of
defence, they would have willingly responded to such
an appeal.   Everywhere I went behind the front lines,
the spirit was excellent among French citizens.   They
would have been prepared to defend their houses and
the streets of their villages, but once they had launched
out from their homes on the unknown adventure of
the great trek southwards, short of food and often
separated from other members of the family, they lost
heart and became liable to waves of panic.   It can also
be argued that unarmed citizens can do little against
well-armed mechanized troops.   That is true, and
everyone would have been wise to remain indoors
when the main body of troops arrived.   They would
have been safer there than on the roads, where they
were liable to be machine-gunned and bombed from
the air, or caught up by mechanized troops, who were
in a hurry to push on and therefore ruthless against
anyone in their way.   On the other hand, these troops

had no time to stop in each French village and hunt among the houses for victims.

Citizens, however, could have been extremely useful in helping to hold up, or cut off, the many individual or small groups of motor-cyclists who dashed ahead at high speed to capture strategic points or to cut communications. They speeded along the straight French roads through deserted country, which was still in the hands of the French, sometimes a day or two days ahead of the main column. Two stories are typical of their methods : French soldiers sitting at the corner of a wood saw a motor-cyclist coming towards them at sixty miles an hour. He slowed up and stopped by them, straddled his legs across the motor-bicycle in the middle of the road and asked to know the way to St. Addresse, a town farther on in French territory. He looked like a German, so they captured him and found that he had instructions on him to be at St. Addresse on that day at a certain hour. When arrested he burst into tears of rage, furious that the French had had the audacity to capture him and prevent his carrying out the Führer's orders. Another German, a policeman, arrived on his motor-bicycle in the middle of the town of Rethel, when it was still in the hands of the French. He had white gloves and a white baton, and orders to arrive at Rethel at the time he did to direct traffic ! All these men had Michelin Guides and went along the French roads as if they were their own, without delaying to reconnoitre and see if the French were still there. Their audacity brought success in the majority of cases,

although many were captured. After the main bodies
of mechanized troops had passed, and before the infantry
arrived, the leading authority in each village could have
called for volunteers to carry out the same work of
sabotage behind the German front lines as the Germans
were carrying out behind the French lines. The risks
run while fighting the enemy in this way are probably
no more than the risks run by those citizens who have
fled but who come eventually under German domination.

Reynaud concluded his " France in Danger " speech
with a phrase which reads tragically now : " These two
great peoples," he said, referring to Britain and France,
" these two Empires, cannot be beaten. France cannot
die. As for me, if I were told to-morrow that only a
miracle could save France, I should reply : ' I believe
in miracles because I believe in France.' " France could
have been saved without miracles. She could have
been saved even as late as May 21 by clear thinking
and courageous decisions on the part of the Government.
But, despite Reynaud's firm words, people with vested
interests continued to have a considerable influence ;
working with the peace party, they undermined the
Prime Minister's authority and eventually gained the
upper hand, persuading the Government to ask for
terms in a vain attempt to save something of their bank
balances, their factories, their houses and their family
life. There were many factors contributing to the
capitulation, but one of the principal ones was the
confusion caused by the refugees. The first definite
order that refugees must not block up the roads and

that they would, if necessary, be held up by the military authorities, was not issued until June 16, a few days before the demand for the German terms and a whole month after the Germans broke through the Meuse. By then it was too late. Having migrated across France, consuming all the spare food and petrol supplies on the way, they were stopped by the Atlantic and collected in a dejected, whispering, poverty-stricken mob round the Government at Bordeaux. The story is told that when an Ambassador went to see Marshal Pétain during those last tragic days at Bordeaux to beg him to carry on the struggle, in North Africa, if necessary, the old man could think of nothing but his pity for the refugees : " We can do nothing," he said ; " all these thousands of people have nowhere to go."

CHAPTER IX

BATTLE OF THE RIVERS

EVENTS were moving rapidly. On May 14 the Dutch Commander-in-Chief had ordered fighting to cease, except in Zeeland, where it continued for a few days ; the German mechanized troops advanced rapidly down the Belgian Meuse and Albert Canal, entering French territory in the Sedan region on May 14 and driving a salient into the French defence lines ; May 16, German mechanized troops crossed the Meuse, through part of the lesser Maginot Line ; May 17, the Germans entered Brussels ; the British Expeditionary Force, with the French Ninth Army and the Belgian forces, had already begun to make their strategic retreat. General Gamelin had issued an order : " Conquer or die," but the German wedge between the Sambre and Sedan continued to widen. A week after the German break-through on the Meuse the country was told the extent of the disaster. " You know," said Reynaud, the Prime Minister, to the Senate, " that the fortifications which were protecting the country can be divided into two parts—the Maginot Line, from Basle to Longwy on the Luxemburg frontier, and the lighter line of fortifications from Longwy to the sea. Holland, Belgium and Luxemburg having been invaded, the left

wing of the French Army advanced from the fortifications between Sedan and the sea, and, pivoting on Sedan,
entered Belgium on a line running from Sedan to
Antwerp and even to Bois-le-Duc in Holland. What
did the enemy do in face of this situation which he
had foreseen and taken into account? He launched a
formidable attack on the pivot of the French Army
established behind the Meuse, between Sedan and
Namur. . . . The pivot of the French Army was
broken and a breach 60 miles wide had been opened
in our front."

Rumours of the disaster, however, had quickly been
circulated in Paris and many of the wealthy began to
leave. There were also changes in the Government
and the High Command which showed that the war
was not going well. On May 18 Reynaud took over
the Ministry of National Defence from Daladier, who
became Foreign Minister, on his way to being dropped
altogether, and Marshal Pétain became Vice-Premier.
The next day General Weygand, who had been Commander-in-Chief of the French Forces in the Near East,
succeeded General Gamelin as Commander-in-Chief of
the Allied Forces. By then the Germans had broken
through the defences on the Oise and Sambre rivers
and had captured Le Cateau and St. Quentin. This
meant that they had advanced 75 miles, as the crow
flies, in four days, striking in from Sedan in a north-
westerly direction and cutting off the nine divisions of
the British Expeditionary Force in the north, with six-
teen of the best French divisions. A large part of the

German mechanized troops turned north in an attempt to cut the Allied forces to pieces; on May 26 they occupied Boulogne and Calais. With the surrender of the Belgian Army at the orders the King of the Belgians, the Allied Forces in the north were in a serious situation and had to fight a desperate retreat along a narrow corridor towards Dunkirk.

During these anxious days the French had made a defensive line along the Somme and the Aisne. It ran roughly from the Channel through Abbeville, Amiens, Peronne and Ham in a south-easterly direction, and then in an easterly direction along the Ailette and Oise rivers by Neufchatel, Rethel and Attigny, continuing east along the Ardennes Canal until it met the Maginot Line proper at Montmédy and Longwy. At the end of May I visited on the Aisne, east of Attigny, a French mechanized division, which had successfully stopped a crack German Panzer division. General Buisson, who was in command, was by nature an extremely confident man. It was almost certainly for that reason that war correspondents were at that critical moment allowed to visit his division. But even he was not too optimistic about the outcome. When the censorship only allows through the optimistic portions of an account given by an optimistic general, a wrong impression is given in the world's press. At that critical moment, when the French needed 'planes from America and mechanized troops and artillery to be re-embarked as quickly as possible from England, the public of the various countries concerned should have been allowed to know how grave was the situation. Into my despatch to London, after visiting General Buisson's division, I included some general comment to show that, while this division was holding a small sector on the Aisne, the situation was not so satisfactory to the west on the Somme. The Panzer division, which had been stopped on the Aisne, was looking for weak points in the defences ; having failed to find them there it had gone westwards towards the Somme. But my general remarks were censored so that the story read, in all the London evening newspapers, as if the French tanks were better than the German and that all was right with the world. The despatch as published in *The Times* of June 1, was as follows :

The French mechanized division which broke the violent attacks of one of the German crack Panzer divisions in tank-to-tank battles and held up the German advance southward from Sedan was visited on Thursday by Reuter's Special Correspondent. He found the officers and men resting by their tanks in concealed ground, after a fortnight of severe fighting. The battle (he says) has developed into classic trench warfare, and at any moment these tank battalions may have to go to the aid of their infantry, after a German attack.

" After fourteen days of fighting we have turned back a Panzer division, and in spite of repeated German mass attacks our one division of infantry has held up two divisions of German infantry, which lost heavily. Since we arrived we have not lost a yard of ground," the general in command declared.

Officers and men who took part said that when the German mechanized columns first broke through the Ardennes in the middle of May the general was ordered to bring up his mechanized division to stop their advance towards the south-west. As soon as they arrived they came face to face with the German heavy tanks, which were followed by lighter tanks accompanying the infantry and escorted by large numbers of aeroplanes.

" It is a new type of tank warfare, like a naval or air battle," the general said. " Our tanks engage the German nose to nose, manœuvring for a flank attack and firing their shells at point-blank range of a few hundred yards. It is all over in a few minutes. Even tanks cannot last under such close-range fire ; they are either sunk or maimed."

A young captain, the son of a well-known general, who alone destroyed twelve German tanks in about as many minutes, said : " We went out with our heavy tanks to meet the Germans, as we heard they were moving to attack. I was separated from the others and suddenly, as I came over the brow of a hill, I found twelve German tanks coming up towards me on the road. The nature of the ground prevented them from manœuvring right or left to outflank me, so we went ahead and knocked one after another on the head in turn. Some caught fire, and all were destroyed with their crews."

There was, however, more to it than that. I had asked the General what would happen if the Germans broke through on the Somme and the Aisne, on what was Weygand's new line. He shrugged his shoulders and refused to answer. He was not going to deny the possibility. " This," he said, " is a mechanical war. It is only with machines that we can beat the enemy. Our soldiers are just as brave as the German, even braver, but it is the machines that win."

That is what the world should have been told : " It is the machines that win." The French General Staff should have learnt it twenty years before, but having failed to realize it until the break through on the Meuse, they should have allowed the world to be told : " unless we get the machines, we are beaten." It was not too late to instruct the Press and the wireless to start a campaign, even when the French were on the Somme and the Aisne. Everyone knew that the French had not got sufficient 'planes or tanks, that the B.E.F. was then embarking at Dunkirk and that it would be some time before the British could send more troops with guns and armoured cars. So what ? The General knew all right, but he was doing his best ; he was by nature a leader and good leaders are optimistic.

The General belonged to what was probably the best unit in the French Army, the Chasseurs. He had previously commanded a Chasseur division and had then been put in command of the mechanized division ; but his old division was still under his command and it was they who had held up two divisions of German infantry.

" The Germans are repeatedly infiltrating through our defences at night along the Aisne," said the General, " but I tell my Chasseurs : ' Whatever happens you must hold your ground,' and, by God ! they do. In the morning, when we come up with a few tanks and drive the Germans back, our men are still there at their posts. The German infantry have been attacking repeatedly and losing heavily, but they are nothing much to write home about. The mechanized division we engaged was a different matter. They were made up of Germany's crack troops and fought very well. We

dealt successfully, however, with this new German
method, which is to use their tanks, not only in support
of infantry, but to work together in squadrons ahead
of the main body of troops cutting as deep into the
country as possible. The German big tanks are about
as heavy as ours, thirty tons, but they have sacrificed
protection to speed; when we can catch them in a
position where they cannot deploy, our tank guns go
through their armour and they are knocked out very
quickly. That is how Captain Billotte managed to bag
his twelve. We destroyed so many of them that they
didn't like it and abandoned their attempt to break
through towards Rheims and Paris."

" In a battle," he continued, " it is extraordinary how
many messengers come to me with wild stories of how
the Germans are breaking through; if sentries have
seen a German advancing they often think that a whole
company is behind him. I tell them that it is nonsense
and that they must go back to have another look. They
generally find that they have made a mistake. One
has to discount all the reports one hears on a field of
battle."

I wondered at the time whether other French commanders had all dealt quite so confidently with the
reports they received on the field of battle. Some of
them, I knew, had been cut off from the main bodies
of their troops and lost contact with other divisions as
a result of the bombing of communications.

" The French troops are getting used to this new
mechanized warfare," continued General Buisson. " The

German air attacks especially took them by surprise when the enemy first broke through on the Meuse. At first even my Chasseurs were disconcerted when the German bombers came over. They go round in a circle, as if dancing a quadrille ; a 'plane dives to within a few feet of the troops, bombs, and rejoins the circle, to be followed by the next and so on, often for half an hour, keeping perfect formation. Even when they have exhausted their bombs, they go on diving at the troops. But they are gradually abandoning the method, as they find it too costly. Our Chasseurs, with their ordinary automatic rifles, have shot down twenty in the last ten days. Once the men at the side of the diving 'planes realized that they could stand or kneel to fire, without being at the 'plane's mercy, they began shooting them down like rabbits."

I asked General Buisson the question that was being asked by everyone at the time : why had it not been possible to stop the mechanized troops, considering how rapidly and how far the enemy were advancing from their bases ; and why had it not been possible to cut the columns ? His answer was in substance as follows. The columns had been cut repeatedly, but that did not prevent more troops arriving ; those tanks and armoured cars which had got through, travelling often at an average speed of 20 miles an hour, had done considerable damage before they were destroyed. The problem was therefore to stop the advance as a whole. In 1917 the Allies had been confronted by the same problem. It was found to be useless to throw one division after

another into the gap ; they were just lost. It was a
question of forming a new defence line in the rear, a
defence line on the Marne, while a rearguard action was
being fought. A minimum of eight days was needed
to form that line ; to bring up troops, guns, ammunition,
supplies ; to make trenches and defensive positions.
In 1917 the Germans had comparatively little mechanized
transport and the advance was at infantry pace, perhaps
5 to 10 miles a day. But in this war the German
mechanized troops were advancing at about 18 miles
a day, and only being kept down to that speed by a
fierce rearguard action. From Sedan to Paris is only
about 125 miles as the crow flies, a distance that could
be covered in seven days, at the reckoning of 18 miles
a day ; Valenciennes, near the Franco-Belgian frontier,
is only 90 miles or five days from Boulogne ; Valenciennes to Amiens on the Somme is only 70 miles or
four days' advance. Fortunately, said the General, the
enemy had had a series of rivers to cross, such as the
Meuse, Oise, Sambre and Ancre. It had been a Battle
of Rivers, and would continue to be so, for they were
the most difficult obstacles for tanks to cross in non-
mountainous country. Defence lines against mechanized
attack had to be stronger and deeper than against infantry
attack, and so took longer to establish. It could be seen,
therefore, that the Allies had not been given much time
to consolidate themselves on the Oise and then on the
Somme. Then again, the Allies should have been able
to bring up troops, guns and supplies more quickly
than in the last war, but transport was held up on the

roads and the railways as a result of the refugees and the constant bombing.

"Our whole trouble," said the General, "is lack of 'planes and tanks."

It was the same complaint as we heard up and down the line. He turned to the American Correspondent who was with us : "You must tell the United States that we need 'planes, more and more 'planes ; they must come ready armed and with their own ammunition."

The Germans had been attacking equally heavily to the west, at Rethel, where I visited an infantry division, commanded by General Delattre, another fine leader. Out of the debris of various French regiments, who were retreating after the break-through on the Meuse, Delattre formed a body of men who held up the German advance towards Rethel long enough for the French to prepare the destruction of the bridges across the Aisne and the digging of defence works. For seven desperate days they held a gap between Château Porcien and Rethel, north of the Aisne, and then continued the fighting in the town. This became known as the Battle of the Cemeteries, for to the north of the town there was both a German and a French cemetery dating from the last war.

The gallant defences put up by Generals de Buisson and Delattre upset the German programme of advance. How minutely it was organized was shown by the capture of the German traffic policeman in Rethel. These policemen were sent ahead to nearly all the big towns in order to help speed up the passage of the mechanized columns. Documents were found on prisoners, who included a Colonel of a Brigade, showing that the German objective was Rheims. After the check on the Aisne, the Germans changed their plans and proceeded in a westerly direction. From all sides there were complaints against Delattre from other commanders, because he had taken their troops. They ignored the fact that Delattre took over these troops, who were mostly stragglers looking for a leader, and by his inspiration made them turn and hold the enemy.

" The best bit of stealing I did," the General told us, " was to capture three French tanks, which had become separated from their unit owing to minor damages. The n.c.o.'s, who were in command of the tanks, agreed to fight with me, and they were magnificent. I don't think we could have held out if it had not been for those three tanks, but I was able to keep them only at the revolver point, because the commander of their unit did everything he could to get them back. The prowess of the three tanks was soon spread in the region and other tanks joined them, so that in a little time we had fourteen tanks ! "

It was a pity that there were not more Delattres in the French Army. Delattre's own division was holding the Aisne farther to the east, over a front of 20 miles, a tremendous distance for 12,000 men to defend.

The General said that the German infantry lost extremely heavily in his sector of the Aisne. In attack they yelled like savages and advanced in the same ecstasy as Arab tribesmen went into battle under Mahomet.

Sometimes whole sections failed to fire, apparently
thinking that their war cries would be sufficient. He
believed that this state was followed by periods of
exhaustion which could be exploited. At the first
attack, 2,500 French shells had been fired within ten
minutes, causing terrible slaughter. There were many
acts of bravery ; a typical one is the story of Lieut.
Gehin's farm. He was a young officer, with English
relations, who had left St. Cyr, the Aldershot of France,
only two months before. He and two of his section,
who had defended the farm, told us their adventure.
His section of twenty-five men had held a farm, north
of the Aisne, from two o'clock in the morning until
two in the afternoon against 400 Germans, who ·had
surrounded them. Two other sections had been in the
farm buildings alongside ; one had been forced to surrender because the granary was burnt down over their
heads, and the other was able to retire. Lieut. Gehin
held on for twelve hours and finally forced the Germans
to withdraw, after their commander and eighty of their
men had been killed. The Germans were all round the
farm, and every now and again their legs could be seen
at the windows as they tried to climb to the storey above.
There was a trench mortar in front, which was so close
that they could hear the range being given, and machine-
guns commanded the building at all points of exit.
Fires in the building were put out as soon as started,
and the French with their machine-guns and rifles kept
the Germans at bay, aided by an artillery barrage from
the French guns in the rear. The Germans retired just

as the French reinforcements were coming to relieve the farm.

With such men to lead and such men to obey, there was no reason why the French should not have held the Germans, even with the discrepancy in 'planes and tanks. Attacks were being launched all along this 120-mile front from the sea to Montmédy, and everywhere the Germans were suffering heavy losses, especially in the Montmédy region, where they repeatedly tried to turn the Maginot Line. But just as the French were beginning to recover their confidence after the breakthrough on the Meuse, and had been able to establish a line of defences, there came, like a thunderclap, the news of the surrender of the Belgian Army at the order of King Leopold. The news of this surrender, announced by Reynaud on the wireless at 8.30 a.m. on May 28, came as a terrible shock to the Army and to the French people. Once more the cry was raised: "We are betrayed," a cry which had been repeated very often after the break-through on the Meuse. Reynaud's announcement was heard in thousands of cafés and homes throughout France. I had just walked into one of those cafés, as the Prime Minister was about to speak. The proprietor was behind the counter; his wife and another woman were at the back of the room. As I sipped my coffee Reynaud began; his first sentence, "I have to inform the French people of a grave event," made the four of us stand rigidly listening. "France," he went on, "can no longer count on the help of the Belgian Army."

There was a gasp from the two women but no one spoke. The voice continued : " The French Army and the British Army are now fighting alone against the enemy in the north. You know what the situation was following the break in our front on May 14. The German Army thrust itself between our armies, which found themselves cut into two groups—one in the north, the other in the south. In the south are French divisions who hold a new front which follows the Somme and the Aisne and then joins up with the intact Maginot Line. In the north is a group of three Allied armies— the Belgian Army, the British Expeditionary Force and some French divisions, among which many of us have a dear one. This group of three armies, under the command of General Blanchard, was supplied via Dunkirk. The French and British armies defended this port in the south and in the west, and the Belgian Army in the north.

" It is this Belgian Army which has, at the height of the battle, unconditionally and without warning its British and French comrades-in-arms, suddenly capitulated on the orders of its King and opened the road to Dunkirk to the German divisions."

The two women burst into tears, crying : " Les salauds, les salauds ! "

Reynaud went on with rasping, bitter phrases : " Eighteen days ago this same King addressed to us an appeal for help. To that appeal we responded, following a plan conceived by the Allied General Staffs last December. Then, when in the midst of battle, King Leopold of the Belgians, who until May 10 always affected to attach as much worth to Germany's word as to that of the Allies, King Leopold III, without warning General Blanchard, without one thought, without one word for the British and French soldiers who came to the help of his country on his anguished appeal, King Leopold III of the Belgians laid down his arms.

" It is a fact without precedent in history.

" The Belgian Government informed me that the King's decision was taken against the unanimous feeling of his responsible Ministers.

" They added that they had decided to put at the service of the common cause all the Belgian forces still at their disposal. Notably, the Belgian Government wishes to raise a new army to collaborate with the French Government.

" It is our soldiers of whom we think. These soldiers can say that their honour is intact. Our soldiers are accomplishing magnificent work at the front every day. During these eighteen days of battle they have given a thousand examples of heroism. The young French generals, who have hardly succeeded their predecessors, are already covering themselves with glory. Our leaders and our soldiers form a bloc in which the country has complete confidence and which will to-morrow be the admiration of the world. We knew that dark days would come, these days have come.

" France has been invaded a hundred times, but never beaten. Let our brave people in the north remember that. It is through these trials that will be forged the new soul of France, a France which will be greater than ever. On the new line which our great leader Weygand, in full accord with Marshal Pétain, has established on the Somme and on the Aisne we shall hold out, and because we shall have held out we shall conquer."

CHAPTER X

WITH THE FRENCH AIR FORCE

"WHERE are our 'planes?" was the cry raised everywhere by French soldiers and by the civilian population. It was difficult not to become demoralized when German 'planes treated the French sky as if it were their own, but the French 'planes were outnumbered by ten to one; they could not be everywhere at once. Unhindered, the Germans bombed communications behind the lines; they bombed troop reinforcements on the road, sometimes succeeding in decimating or dispersing regiments before they ever reached the front line; they swept down over the heads of the men at the front; they bombed the towns and villages of France and they bombed and machine-gunned refugees on the road.

The French Air Command wanted the world, especially America, to know how serious the situation was, and towards the end of May war correspondents were received at Chantilly by the General commanding the northern air sector and two other Air Generals. Each gave a very interesting lecture about what the French Air Force was doing, and all emphasized this discrepancy of ten to one. Unfortunately, whenever I put these figures into a story they were crossed out by the censor !

The French Air Force personnel were excellent, except perhaps for a few units, but their 'planes were very much slower than the German. The Morane chasers had very little chance against the Messerschmitts; it was only towards the end that American machines were arriving in any number. Each army had its own squadron of fighter, 'planes for the protection of the troops, but there were not enough of them, and, following the bombing carried out by the Germans on May 10, there were fewer still. The day that Holland, Belgium and Luxemburg were invaded the Germans bombed France for the first time. They knew exactly where every aerodrome was, and they attacked the majority at dawn on May 10. I was at Nancy at the time, where they bombed the town, after destroying at least ten 'planes at the Toul aerodrome nearby; there were similar losses at aerodromes all over France. After that the French air-fields were being repeatedly attacked, and repeatedly changed. This caused disorganization at a time when chasers and bombers were especially needed to work to the utmost. One of the officers in charge of the aerodrome at Chartres described the difficulties:

" Each time we move to a new air-ground, which we do about every two or three days, the ground staff have to follow us either by train or lorry. Owing to the heavy bombing of communications there are very few trains and on the roads everyone is held up because of the refugees, with the result that the staff often arrive at the air-grounds after we have already left for a new destination. Our crews, who are already exhausted by long hours of flying, have to do all the work of reloading the bombs, refuelling and general maintenance. We sometimes don't even have the right tools for dealing with bombs after they are taken from the packing cases. No one can carry out repeated and intensive bombing of the enemy under such conditions.

" Besides that, several of our crews, who have had to jump for it, have landed in completely deserted country, as a result of the evacuation by the civilian population, and often take days to return to their base. I had to jump with my crew after bombing Montcornet; we landed safely, but there was not a living human being in sight, only the cows munching placidly in the fields. We walked for some hours along a road, passing through villages where there was no one to direct us, or lend us even a bicycle. At last we found a village where there was one old man, who had decided to stay even if the Germans came. I have seldom been so pleased to see anyone as that old man, for, by showing us where we could find bicycles, we were able to get back to our base before it moved off again. If it had not been for him we should probably still be walking along."

During those days towards the end of May, when war correspondents were being kept from the front, one of the best ways of finding out what was happening was to visit the air squadrons. I had made friends with a charming French Air Officer, Colonel François, commanding a night bombing squadron at Nangis, east of Paris. He allowed me to see his maps, which gave the position of the enemy lines every evening. The maps were on a big scale and covered the entire wall in one of the rooms, so that one could get a very good idea how the battle was progressing. Each evening the new German line was marked in and the old one, some way in the rear, was rubbed out. At about 6 p.m. the orders came through for that night's operations. They were always short and to the point, stating the objectives ; the itinerary ; number and weight of bombs, and the points to be noted by the observer. As we were studying the map with the Colonel and the crews, who were going up that night, I thought what a good story it would be if I could go and bomb the enemy lines. I did not think that there was much chance of doing so, for there was a very strict order that no journalist could go up in a fighting 'plane ; no one had been able to get round that, but if anyone did go up, it certainly would not happen again, so that it would be an exclusive story. I turned and asked the Colonel :

" May I go up to-night ? "

" Why not ? " he said.

" You really mean it ? "

" Certainly."

I went out to the car to get a bottle of cognac, for I felt that this deserved a little celebration. I was to be the only journalist to go on a bombing mission. Taylor Henry of the Associated Press had come with me, but fortunately he considered that it might cause trouble if he, an American, went and bombed the Germans. I appreciated his scruples. But poor Henry was miserable for the rest of the evening, torn between his conscience and his desire to go up. The idea of interviewing me after I had returned from the expedition did not appeal to him. In fact he was so gloomy that we decided that some way round the problem must be found. I suggested that he should say that he had flown in a reconnaissance 'plane and describe what he saw. He thought this was possible and cheered up considerably. The difficulty was that the Colonel did not want him to go up, because he thought there might be complications over it. We went into the mess and had a very pleasant dinner. The Colonel came from the Ardennes, where his squadron had continually bombed German troop concentrations during the break-through on the Meuse in the middle of May. For the third time his old father of 76 had seen the Germans invade France. He had been there in 1870, 1914 and 1940. François was revenging from the air an age-old feud between the two peoples. He was delighted that he had been the first French pilot to bomb a German town, after the enemy had bombed Nancy and other places in France.

"Why we weren't allowed to do it before, I don't know!" he said. "I was told to bomb the air-field outside the town and return, but I wasn't going to come back without bombing the town as well!"

He had become a well-known character to the Germans and had on several occasions been the subject of bitter attacks on the German wireless. It is a pity that orders were not disobeyed more often in this way.

He knew the Belgians well and said that he did not trust them at all. Before the war he had been working on the French Air Staff and had been on a mission into Belgium. It had been of little value because the Belgian Staff had refused to tell the French officers any of their plans or even reveal the disposition of their aerodromes. We did not know then that, even while we were talking at dinner, King Leopold had decided to order his army to surrender. As a former member of the French Staff the Colonel had bitter things to say about French politicians over the past ten years and their inability to realize the need for more 'planes.

Another member of the mess was Gaston Pavlevski, Reynaud's able Chef de Cabinet when the latter had been Minister of Finance. There had been a quarrel with Daladier, then Prime Minister, who had forced Pavlevski to resign. Pavlevski's plan was to serve for some months with the fighting forces, to return to Paris with the best war record of any civil servant, and to be given a high post by Reynaud, who had become Prime Minister. He had achieved the first part of his plan, as he had been given the Croix de Guerre for the good work he had carried out with the squadron as observer. I believe the second part of his ambition would also have been fulfilled, but events moved too quickly.

At nine o'clock some of the officers, who were to carry out the first bombings, left the table. We sat on and drank a little more wine and cognac, which Henry and I had presented to the mess. It made me

feel a little more optimistic than I would otherwise have
done. I found myself thinking of the information I
had noted down when I had first arrived at the aerodrome
in the afternoon. Twenty-five per cent. of the crews
had been lost, since the German invasion of France a
fortnight before. I had listened to stories of young
pilots who had had to jump for their lives out of
burning 'planes. One pilot had nearly been caught
because the man who jumped before him had pulled
his parachute cord too soon and it had opened in the
'plane ; the pilot had just managed to kick it free and
to jump himself when the 'plane was only a thousand
feet from the ground. I thought, too, of the large holes
which I had seen being mended in the 'planes by the
men they called " The First Aid Corps."

" Oh, yes," an airman had said, as I looked at some
of the holes, which were as big as a man's body, " Fritz
has some good anti-aircraft guns. He makes it pretty
hot for us whenever we go over."

With the prospect of going up in an hour's time,
these young men seemed to me even braver than they
had at the time they told me their stories.

" By the way," said the Colonel, " you had better
leave behind any notes you have taken, just in case you
are caught." He looked at me reflectively for a moment
and added : " As you are in uniform you ought to be
all right, if you do fall into their hands."

The brandy came round again and I filled my glass
as full as possible. Taylor Henry, on the other side of
the Colonel, was using all his persuasive French, tinged

with an American accent, to break down the opposition
to his going. By the time coffee arrived he had achieved
his end. We went back to headquarters, where I put
on a spare flying suit belonging to the Colonel, and
we were on the air-ground at midnight when the first
air missions were returning. They reported that they
had successfully bombed their objectives in spite of the
darkness of the night. I was to go up with Colonel
François and we sat together under a wing of the 'plane,
watching the bombs being loaded. It took two men
to carry the hundred-pounders across the field to the
'plane, and four men, standing in a pit underneath, to
manœuvre these four-foot bombs into place. All the
time the beacon on the air-field was flashing the code
word to show the way to the returning 'planes, and the
big lorries could be heard moving from one part of
the air-field to another, busy refuelling.

By about 12.20 a.m. everything was ready and my
parachute was buckled on. I was told that if I had to
jump I must count ten before pulling the clasp on the
left of the belt. Taylor Henry was also equipped ready
to go with the 'planes, which were to bomb the Cambrai
air-field. The Colonel's group was to bomb a big
cross-roads outside Bapaume, where German troops
were massed. We climbed into the old Amiot ; seven
years old, and with a maximum speed of 125 m.p.h.
They explained that they could not use these old machines
in daytime, owing to their slowness, and therefore put
them on the night shifts. Once again I was forced to
admire the Frenchman's sense of economy ; but I looked

longingly towards the new, fast Amiots, which were being used that night for deep reconnaissance work over Germany.   There was only room for a sleeping partner like myself in one of the old machines.

I settled down in the second pilot's seat and the crew of three climbed in. The navigator and bomber was in front of me ; the Colonel climbed up into the pilot's seat above my head, while the wireless operator and machine-gunner went to his post in the rear of the 'plane. The navigator explained to me that, if I liked, he would attach the cord of my parachute to a clip above my head, which would open it automatically if we had to jump. I said I thought it would be a very good idea, but it was not put into effect, for at that moment the Colonel called to him, and a few moments later there was a shout of " Contact made, stand clear," and the engines were started up with a roar. Not a light was to be seen, except for the flash of the beacon and the occasional light of the navigator's torch as he arranged his maps. We moved slowly over the air-field, took up our position, and started our dash across the field. Slowly we mounted to 5,000 feet and proceeded steadily along through the dark night. It was as uneventful as a ride in a London omnibus, but less comfortable, for I had to sit bolt upright, like a mid-Victorian, since the bulky parachute stuck into my back. There was glass both sides of the 'plane, and soon I could see the silver bends of the Marne below. Roads could only be distinguished when a car passed, and then I was surprised to notice how clearly they were shown up. After about an hour's flight I could see St. Quentin aflame on the right, and, farther north, was the light of burning Cambrai, where I still, theoretically, had a room reserved in the station hotel, with my clothes hanging up in the cupboard. To the left was another large fire which I was told was Amiens burning. I wondered what had happened to the fine Cathedral, which had escaped so miraculously in the last war, but I was told afterwards by another pilot, who had flown over the Cathedral by day, that the fires were in farm buildings outside the town and that the Cathedral was untouched. On the horizon were flashes of artillery fire. It was perhaps the beginning of the big French counter-offensive, which I knew had been planned for that night.

The navigator came over and shouted to me that we were over the German lines. I looked out each side to see if there was any sign of anti-aircraft fire, but all was dark, except for a line of lights, probably those of a convoy, which went out as we roared overhead. The wireless operator informed us that a German chaser had been after us, firing its machine-gun ; but we had escaped it. How, I do not know, considering the speed that we were going. I think it was probably a figment of the operator's imagination, but at the time it made me finger my parachute clip anxiously, wondering whether I would have the presence of mind to pull it at the right moment, as I charged headlong down towards the Germans. That wait of ten seconds might so easily be drawn into eternity. The navigator came over again and pulled triggers over my head.

" I am getting ready for the bombing," he shouted.
He was beginning to get excited, flashing his torch
at the map and repeatedly communicating with the pilot
through the rubber speaking-tube. He had set the
bombs to fall fifty yards apart, and all was now ready.
He turned to me and pointed downwards, as he held
what looked like a revolver at the end of a tube. The
great moment had come. The bombs had been released
and I was gazing intently downwards, but I saw absolutely
nothing. For all I could tell we might have been raining
dud bombs on Brighton, instead of dropping hundred-
pounders on German troop concentrations at Bapaume,
perhaps killing forty or fifty people as they slept. It
was all curiously impersonal at 5,000 feet. The navigator
came and shouted :

" I hit the cross-roads all right ; I suppose you saw
the bombs explode ? "

I nodded assent. After all their kindness to me, I
could not let them down by saying that I had missed
the *pièce de résistance*. As we turned back he pointed
over towards Cambrai to what he said were puffs of
smoke above the aerodrome, made by the bombs being
dropped by the other group of 'planes. I nodded again.
Only a week before I had seen the Germans bombing
the same air-field, and the French fighters going up
after them. I realized that it needs a lot of training to
make a good observer and a good pilot for night flying.
The Germans had been making it even harder for the
observers by planting lights all over the fields, to give
the impression of a small town, and so put the pilot

off his course. But these crews knew their ground so well that they were never taken in, and if there was any doubt they dropped a parachute flare, which showed up these artificial towns. On our return journey, the pilot dropped one of the flares and the whole countryside below us was lit up. This was in order to enable the observer to carry out one of his instructions, which was to look out for German troop movements. The enemy were in the habit of rushing up troops under cover of darkness. Everything was still, however, and even the observer could see no movement.

When we had returned, the Colonel said that it was the first time in the squadron's experience that the Germans had held their fire, and he thought that it might be due to the fact that they had learnt of the planned counter-offensive and did not want to reveal new gun positions. By the time we had reached the good hard ground again, I was sorry that there had not been more excitement.

The flight had taken a little over two hours, and by the time we got back to headquarters it was 2.30 in the morning. I was anxious to know what adventures Taylor Henry had had over Cambrai. He was waiting for me when I arrived, but I could see at once that something was wrong. Alas, poor Henry ! His 'plane had had engine trouble and he had not been able to leave.

We went to bed for a short time, getting up early to go to another air-base about 50 miles away. After lunch in the mess we visited the air-field and talked to

the pilots taking part in dive bombing. This method
of attack, which had been used so much by the Germans
at first, was now being used less by them and more by
the French. The pilots said that the heavier, retarded
bombs, dropped at an altitude of a hundred feet or so,
caused great havoc. On hard surfaces the bombs took
three or four leaps over a distance of about a quarter
of a mile before exploding, and when dropped down
a straight road after troops they had a big effect.

I had told Henry that, if he liked, I would drive him
back to Nangis to see if he could get his flight that
night. Unfortunately it was raining heavily, but we
decided to try all the same and reached Nangis at 8 p.m.
We went into dinner at the hotel and could see that
the squadron was at mess next door. We had taken
the precaution of sending in another bottle of cognac
as a sign we were there, and Henry had telephoned a
friendly captain, who said he would take him up if it
were possible. At 10 p.m. there was still no response
from next door and Henry had given up hope. We
ordered two bottles of good burgundy to drown his
sorrow. As we were finishing the second bottle, in
walked the Colonel, who said cheerfully :

" Well, are you coming up to-night ? "

Off we went again. This time I sat in the rear and
had charge of a machine-gun. I am doubtful if I would
have been able to fire it successfully if a chaser 'plane
had come our way, for I had been helping to drown
Henry's sorrows to some effect. Everything was explained to me very carefully and I felt confident that

I would be able to bring down any number of Messer-schmitts. I felt more at ease in the open turret with the machine-gun, as it would have been easy to climb out if there had been any need to jump. The previous night, when I had been in the body of the 'plane, I had wondered who would be expected to go out of the exit first, and whether there would be that same business of polite bowings, which habitually delays a group of Frenchmen at every door they wish to pass through. This time we dropped no bombs.

It was fortunate that I had brought Henry back to do his flight, for otherwise I should never have got my story through the censorship. When we returned to Paris and gave in our stories there was at first a tremendous outcry. The Air censors at the Hotel Continental said that Colonel François knew perfectly well that no journalists were allowed to fly and that he would get into serious trouble for having allowed us to do so. The matter was reported to General Vuillemin, Commanding the French Air Force, while Henry and myself appealed to our respective embassies, firstly to try to stop François getting into trouble and secondly to get the story through. The British Embassy said they thought that it was good, live propaganda, and that they would, if necessary, see Reynaud himself on the matter. I could not have asked for anything better. But, as usual, there was a hitch ; someone had advised caution, and I was told the next day that it was thought wiser not to interfere in French military matters, and that the matter had been dropped. Bullitt, the American

Ambassador, however, took the matter up, and the story was allowed to go through.

My impressions after visiting seven or eight air-bases was that the French were well-trained and courageous pilots, even though they had not got the same dash as the R.A.F., but their 'planes were on the whole not as fast as the German, and they were heavily outnumbered. The French military authorities were generous in allowing so much publicity to the Royal Air Force, both in the official communiqués and in the Press, and I do not think that sufficient was said about the courage and ability of the French pilots in flying inferior machines against such odds. I saw the day-to-day reports of numerous squadrons ; there were cases in which three French 'planes had engaged eight German ; five had engaged twelve and so on. I never saw a case where the enemy had been inferior in number. The French pilots were certainly respected by the German, for whenever there were six French 'planes together, the Germans nearly always avoided fighting, even if they were treble the number. There was the work, too, of the reconnaissance 'planes, which almost every day flew over enemy territory to take photographs. The services were well organized, with mobile photographic vans developing and printing hundreds of photographs daily. These series of vertical photographs, taken from the air and fitted together to cover many square miles of country, were very interesting, though it needed an extremely well-trained eye to be able to interpret them. The line maps, which were drawn from the photographs, gave the interpretations of the various marks of light and shade, which to me conveyed very little, but the photo detective found gun emplacements, fortifications, oil reserves, barracks and even troops drilling, which was invaluable information for the bombing squadrons and for the General Staff. With the stereoscopic photographs, that is, two of the same area taken from different angles, it was possible, with the stereoscopic lens, to distinguish much more. Fortifications and houses, which had been merely flat shadows, suddenly jumped into prominence.

The prowess of the various squadrons varied considerably ; and the differences generally depended upon the type of officer who was in command. The best squadrons were those led by an officer who was himself still an active pilot. There were, it is true, some squadrons where the spirit was not sufficiently aggressive. With Eddie Ward of the B.B.C. I visited an air-base near Evreux, at the beginning of June, when the Germans had begun to break through on the Somme and the Aisne, and were making for the Seine. It was naturally extremely important that the French bombers should be as active as possible, bombing the enemy troop concentrations and lines of communications. We were in the Colonel's office when the General commanding the Air Unit telephoned to say that orders had come through from headquarters that waves of bombers must be sent immediately to harry the advancing enemy. We could hear him giving his orders in a loud voice down the telephone. It was essential, he said, that

certain objectives must be bombed immediately. The
Colonel was very firm that nothing could be done for
at least another two hours. The General had to accept
that, but he was not pleased. The squadron went off
at the appointed time and Ward stayed to see them
return ; I had to motor back to Paris. The Air Force
officers took Ward out to the field, saying that they
wanted him to see a bombing mission, so that he could
describe it in his broadcast ; he would be able to talk
to the pilots and find out what they had done. This
was exactly what Ward wanted. He talked to the first
lot of pilots who came in : they had had very bad
visibility and could not find their objectives, so had
returned without dropping any bombs. The next lot
had met Messerschmitts and had decided to turn about
without dropping their bombs ; and so it was with all
of them. If Colonel François had been in command
of that squadron I am sure that all those bombs would
have been dropped somewhere over the German lines,
and he would, at such a moment of crisis, been leading
the squadrons, instead of sitting in an office.

CHAPTER XI

THE BATTLE FOR FRANCE

THE month of May turned into June and the brilliant summer weather, which was such an advantage to the enemy's mechanized columns and air force, continued day after day. France waited breathlessly to learn the result of the fighting round Dunkirk, for they knew that once the Germans had reached the coast, they would recommence their drive towards Paris. Hitler had generally announced his objectives beforehand with a violent air bombardment, and, on June 3, Paris was bombed for the first time, over 250 people being killed. The bombing occurred at 1.30 in the afternoon and I did not reach the capital until 3.30 p.m., as I was returning from a visit to the Maginot Line with Jerome Willis of *The Evening Standard*. We had seen the German 'planes go over and learnt that Paris had been bombed on our way into the capital, but when we arrived it took us a little time to find out what had been bombed. No one in the Place St. Michel seemed to know, when we stopped there for a drink. Finally we found someone who had heard a report that the Renault and Citroën works had been hit. We dashed out there to find the former untouched but the Citroën works badly damaged. The roads leading there were crowded with visitors, and I was surprised to see that little attempt was made to check them wandering about among the hundreds of firemen busy at work. I was able to go in and out of the buildings, take photographs and ask as many questions as I wanted ; only once did anyone ask for my papers. One of the first to arrive was a member of the Italian Embassy, who made a thorough examination of the damage and then, presumably, telegraphed to his Government. About a hundred 'planes came over Paris and scored direct hits with heavy bombs of 200 lbs. and more over nearly the entire length of the works, which cover about a quarter of a mile. At one end there was only a wall left standing precariously. The roof of the vast garage had gone and fires were burning. Farther along, there were huge stretches of glass which had been blown out, but the framework of the roof remained intact as the blast of the bombs had been able to escape. The administrative premises beyond had been heavily damaged by a series of direct hits. The workshops and garages had contained a number of cars, but there was no attempt to drive them away until about twenty minutes after the fires had started. An R.A.F. officer, who arrived soon after the 'planes had passed, drove several cars into safety himself. The fire engines took half an hour to arrive. Fortunately all the workmen had been still out at their midday meal, otherwise the death-roll would have been very heavy. They had gone down into the shelters and had not come out until the " all clear " had been sounded. By that time most of the cars had been driven out by bystanders. The damage elsewhere in Rue Pasteur, Quai Louis Blériot (if he had only known how his enterprise was to be exploited !), was very similar to what I had seen in Nancy, Vouziers, Vitry-le-François and many other towns. At one corner of the Rue Pasteur, which was a smart residential quarter, a bomb had dropped through six storeys, exploding at the bottom and tearing out every floor, except the sixth, which remained intact but for the hole where the bomb had passed. At the time that the bomb fell, a man and a woman had been coming down the staircase to go to the shelter. The staircase was cut at the fifth floor ; they were unhurt, but remained suspended in mid-air on the staircase until firemen rescued them. No one, who went into the cellars or shelters in time, was injured, but the sirens had sounded only a few minutes before the 'planes arrived, so that many were caught out in the streets or in their houses.

Reynaud announced in a broadcast in the evening that the Citroën factories were working normally that night, but I visited them after midnight, and, as far as I could see, the whole place was still occupied by firemen. It would, in fact, have been very unwise to continue work as a number of unexploded bombs were still buried in the ground floor.

The next day I left with a number of other war correspondents for the Aisne front. Every 500 yards near the front line we passed barricades across the roads, built of huge blocks of stone, old Fords, ploughshares and anything that there was to hand. Many of them were guarded by negro troops from Equatorial Africa, who had dealt very effectively with the Germans during the last war, but in the war of 1940 they had little chance of getting to grips with the enemy, and were frightened by the noise of the 'planes and the sight of the tanks.   On July 5 we arrived near the Aisne to the north-west of Soissons.   We were on our way to visit an observation post looking out on the German lines. Before getting there we were stopped at a farm, which had been bombed a few hours before and a haystack was burning.   It seemed little damage enough, but I was told that the enemy do their best to set haystacks on fire, as they burn for several days and make a good guide for 'planes.   Telephone lines were down there, as elsewhere, for the second big German offensive had been launched that morning, and the lines of communications were, as usual, being cut.   The Press Lieutenant, who was in charge of us, tried to arrange that we should go forward, but the Army we were visiting was engaged in battle, and headquarters did not want to bother about a group of journalists.

This was the beginning of what Reynaud described as the Battle for France.   The " Weygand Line," built on the principle of defence in depths, was as good as it had been possible to make it in the short time that the Germans had allowed.   It was not thought that the enemy could launch a second big offensive so soon after the first, especially considering the distances that they had covered, and the fact that they had also made a drive towards the Channel ports.

Half a million infantry, supported by nearly 1,000
'planes, were employed in the attack, which started at
4 a.m. on June 5 with heavy artillery preparation.   On
the 120-mile front the three main thrusts were in the
region of Amiens, Peronne and the Aillette Canal,
towards the main roads leading to Paris.   The enemy
were following out the von Schlieffen plan, thrusting
past Amiens and the lower Somme in an enveloping
movement towards the south-west of Paris.   In the
centre the enemy were to cut through by Compiègne
down the valley of the Oise directly towards Paris ;
further to the east the Germans were to cross the Aisne
in the direction of the Marne Valley, thus closing the
pincer movement on the capital.

" It is Germany's most decisive enterprise," said Reynaud in a broadcast speech.   " It is an attack in grand
style preceded by a proclamation by Hitler to his troops.
All the means of which we know have been put into
operation.   Aircraft and armoured divisions are once
more attempting an infiltration and a break-through of our
front.   All the world watches breathlessly the develop-
ment of this battle, because the battle of June, 1940, will
decide its fate, as Hitler has said, perhaps for centuries."

War correspondents were now confined to Paris, and
were not allowed to see anything of one of the greatest
battles in history.   We had to content ourselves with the
morning and evening conferences of Colonel Thomas,
the tall, bespectacled spokesman of the War Office.
Instead of taking place as usual at the Ministry of National
Defence, the conference was held in the ornate Clock

Room at the Quai d'Orsay, where the Briand-Kellogg Peace Pact had been signed to banish war as an instrument for furthering national ends. The big room with its conference table down the middle was full of journalists on the evening of June 5. All sat tensely listening as the Colonel announced : "To-day has begun the greatest battle of the war ; we cannot yet tell what the result will be." Each morning and evening we went to listen to Colonel Thomas, who was our only contact with the battle-front, so soon to approach the gates of Paris. Thomas had been rather ridiculed the first eight months of the war, when he tried to give life to the communiqués which kept on proclaiming : "Nothing to report." But now we clung to Thomas ; we followed every inflexion of his voice, every gesture, in the hope of catching some special significance. Every word was carefully written down ; when he had concluded there was a rush to the newspaper offices and his words were flashed to every corner of the world. His importance to us grew from day to day as the Battle for France waged fiercer and fiercer. In his quiet voice he announced the numbers of those engaged ; the first day, tanks were hardly mentioned ; the second day it was stated that the Germans had thrown in every tank they had, about 2,000 in all ; on the third day there was a gasp in the Clock Room as Thomas calmly stated that the Germans had thrown 4,000 tanks into the battle. The ten divisions that he had mentioned as the German attacking force during the first day of the battle suddenly jumped to nearly 100 divisions, about 2,000,000 men.

The French man-in-the-street was bewildered:
"What!" he said, "4,000 tanks and nearly 100
divisions! It is unbelievable! Yesterday we were told
they only had 2,000 tanks."

But there was still a further blow to fall on already
stricken France. Italy declared war. "The hour
marked out by destiny is sounding in the sky of our
country," declared Mussolini on June 10. "This is the
hour of irrevocable decisions. The declaration of war
has already been handed to the Ambassadors of Britain
and France. We are going to war against the plutocrats
and reactionary democracies of the west, who have
hindered the advance and often threatened the existence,
even, of the Italian people." That was the bitterest blow
of all to the French. The Italians, whom they knew
that they could defeat in battle, were to despoil them, if
there should be a German victory.

"It is at this very moment," cried Reynaud, "when
France, wounded but valiant and undaunted, is fighting
against German hegemony for her own independence,
as well as for that of the whole world, that Mussolini
has chosen to declare war on us. . . . We are in the
sixth day of the greatest battle in history. Our soldiers,
our airmen and the Royal Air Force have been facing an
enemy superior in numbers and armaments. In this
war, which is no longer a war of continuous fronts, but
a war of strong points grouped in depth, our armies have
been manœuvring in retreat. They did not abandon
any strong point until they had inflicted cruel losses on
the enemy. The kilometres gained by the enemy are

scarred by destroyed tanks and by 'planes brought down."

By then German troops had already crossed the Seine at various points south of Rouen. By Sunday night, June 9, all the Government departments had packed up and had left the capital. Reynaud had gone to Weygand's headquarters. It became all the more imperative for journalists to find out what was happening. On Monday morning, June 10, we all waited as usual for Colonel Thomas in the Clock Room at the Quai d'Orsay. For nine and a half months he had always been punctual for every conference, but on that morning he never arrived. He had already left Paris. Everyone from the Ministry of Information and from the other Government offices had left Paris, although up to the last moment they had announced that they would remain, whatever happened. Colonel Thomas, our last link with the battle, had departed. The man we had depended on so long had vanished in the night. There was nothing left for us but to follow the Government to Tours or to stay in Paris as long as possible before the Germans arrived, without any knowledge of where they were or how fast they were advancing. We knew that the French line had broken, so that, if the Germans kept up their usual rate of progress, there was no reason why they should not be in Paris that same day.

The best account of what the Germans were doing in the meantime is given in one of their own High Command reports, which were soberly and accurately written, for, as Mr. Noel Baker remarked in a recent article : " Hitler's passion for war is so great that it is the only subject on which he tells the truth." The report states : " Hardly had the annihilating battle in Flanders and Artois been terminated, when our Air Force and Army proceeded to the second decisive blow against the French, using many divisions, which had not yet seen battle. The new operations were opened on June 3 by air attacks on the aerodromes and aviation industries round Paris, which had destructive effect. On the next day three Army Corps stood ready under the command of General von Brauchitsch. The objective of the new operations was to break through the French northern front, to throw back the separated French Armies to the south-west and the south-east and thereupon to destroy these armies. When the divisions of the Army Corps, commanded by General von Boch, launched the attack on June 5 over the lower Somme and Oise–Aisne canal, they were confronted by an enemy prepared for defence. The French Command was resolved, with the use of all available forces, to defend to the last the ' Weygand Line ' and the Maginot Line. After a severe struggle of four days the infantry and armoured divisions broke through the enemy front.

On June 9, the pursuit was in full course towards the lower Seine and in the direction of Paris. Mechanized troops, under the command of Infantry General Hoth, reached Rouen on the same day in a headlong advance, which resulted in the enemy being surrounded on the coast near Dieppe, and their left wing being shattered. The Air Force helped considerably in the break-through on the Seine ; enemy infantry and tank divisions were dispersed by our bombs, while they were assembling for a counter-attack. By cutting railway lines and destroying railway material, the Air Force robbed the enemy of the possibility of moving up reserves and throwing them into the gap, where the break-through had occurred. As soon as the first signs of embarcations of troops at Havre, Cherbourg and Brest were noted, our Air Force successfully attacked ports, oil reservoirs and ships."

The report goes on to describe the break-through on the Aisne " in heavy fighting, which lasted two days against an enemy who defended himself to the utmost."

France was dazed by the rapidity of the enemy successes. Soldiers and citizens did not know where to turn. But there was one card still left to play, which might have saved the country—the defence of Paris.

CHAPTER XII

PARIS COULD HAVE BEEN DEFENDED

DURING that last week-end it was announced that Paris had been placed in a state of defence. What that meant it was difficult to know. If the French authorities had really intended to defend Paris they should have appealed to the citizens to aid in the defence of their capital, helping the soldiers to build barricades along every street. Volunteer corps should have been formed and strong defensive positions chosen in the capital, with stores of food and ammunition ready, so that they could hold out even if surrounded. With such an appeal, and with good use made of the wireless, the face of the capital would have been changed. Instead of wandering about like frightened sheep wondering how they were to get away, citizens would have been busy with the defence of Paris. The main stronghold would have been, as it has been in the past, the steep hill of Montmartre. Anti-aircraft guns could have been taken up to the top to keep off the low-flying 'planes, and the streets leading up the hill could have been barricaded. Out-posts could have been posted on the Arc de Triomphe, the Château of Vincennes, in the region of the Observatory at Montparnasse and at other commanding positions. There was already a well-armed police force; there were the many hundreds of workers at the Renault and Citroën works, there were the porters at the Halles markets, and there were many British, American, Czech, Poles and other nationals who would have enthusiastically joined in the defence. Units of the dismembered armies, who had been fighting on the Seine and the Aisne, and who were still eager to fight, would have found their way to Paris as a rallying centre; many of the artillery would have been able to bring their guns. Madrid has shown what a determined defence can do; the Republicans kept off attacks from Italian 'planes and German tanks for many months. In Warsaw a mechanized German division was turned back by Polish snipers. Tanks are at a disadvantage fighting in a town; while delayed at the barricades they can be put out of action with grenades and "molotoff cocktails" flung from the houses on both sides; in a few minutes the crews are suffocated by the heat and the tank remains to strengthen the barricade. There were men who had fought in the International Brigade, and who were not such fervent upholders of the Third International that they would not have defended their own capital. They should have been told to organize the street fighting on the lines they had learnt in Spain, even if they had to be brought out of prison to do it. France only needed leaders and a rallying ground in order to recover her fighting spirit. Once the news spread that Paris was defending itself, every town which was still free of the Germans would have prepared to hold out; Lyons,

Dijon, Troyes, Le Mans, Orleans and hundreds of others could have put up a stout resistance. Every town and village would have been a rallying ground for infantry and artillery soldiers who had lost their units. The French are brilliant improvisers ; they would have had full scope in the towns, whereas in the open country they had not had the time to make their defensive lines. Reynaud had said : " This is no longer a war of continuous fronts, but a war of strong points grouped in depths." The towns of France would have been those strong points, and the blocks of houses at every street corner would have been the strong points in the towns. The French Army, and there were several divisions which had not yet engaged in battle, would perhaps have had time to make a defensive line along the Loire, or, if not, they could have defended the Massif Central in the Clermont Ferrand region. Britain, instead of withdrawing the three divisions, which had been fighting on the Somme, would have rushed over new troops. Despite the German 'planes they would have forced a landing on the west coast of France. Another British Expeditionary Force had been on the way, but was turned back when it was known that Paris had been declared an open town. France would have had sufficient arms and ammunition to defend these strong points. Anti-aircraft guns could have been installed over the Renault works, so that it might continue to turn out armaments. American 'planes were already arriving in large numbers ; their despatch would have been speeded up and arms and ammunition would have

been sent, once it was known that France had rallied—
that she had found her old vitality for self-preservation
and was determined to fight to the bitter end.

That is what Reynaud and de Gaulle would have
done. France would have understood a *levée en masse* ;
it was in her revolutionary tradition. The people had
not been appealed to as individuals, they had only been
ordered about as soldiers, and the civilians had had
no orders at all, except not to eat meat or drink alcohol
on certain days of the week. They had not been treated
as intelligent human beings. Unfortunately France had
leaders more afraid of a popular movement than of
Hitler succeeding. Men like Weygand, Pétain, and
several others in the Cabinet, were dominated by the
fear of a Communist uprising. The fact that the Left
and the Extreme Left were, in the main, good patriots,
before they were members of the Third International,
did not come into the question. The Government did
not want the men at the Renault works and the other
citizens of Paris to fight. They had even given orders
to the police to fire on them if they showed any sign of
defending the capital.

Reynaud had failed to dominate the peace party,
who feared a revolution and had made up their minds
to capitulate. Besides that, there was the pressure of
those with large vested interests, who shrank from the
idea of Paris being bombarded and their beautiful
buildings and their homes being destroyed. They had
not the stomach to say with regard to France what
Churchill said with regard to England : " We shall

defend every village, every town and every city. The vast mass of London, fought street by street, could easily devour an entire hostile army, and we would rather see London laid in ruins and ashes than that it should be tamely and abjectly enslaved. . . .

"But Hitler has not yet been withstood by a great nation with a will-power equal to his own. Many of these countries have been poisoned by intrigue. They have been rotten from within before they were smitten from without. How else can you explain what has happened in France, to the French Army, to the French people, and to the leaders of the French people?"

It is a severe condemnation, all the more severe that it comes from someone who has known France and defended her. But it is wrong to interpret it as meaning that France has ceased for all time to be a vital nation, that she is decadent and finished, as the Germans and Italians have argued. The rank and file of the French Army and the French people were not rotten from within, but the political system was rotten and it produced leaders, with a few exceptions, who were not fit to lead a great nation. If she had been well led, France would have shown as much vitality as she has done during previous national emergencies. It is as true to say that leaders produce the kind of nation that they want to produce, as to say that a nation deserves the leaders it gets. French individualism, which is an all too vigorous growth, kept the nation playing with a bad political system overlong, and by the time that danger was at her gates, she had no longer the power to revolt against her leaders. Five million of her men were mobilized prisoners of the French General Staff, and a rigid censorship kept the public ignorant of the issues involved. Any argument, however, about the degree of rottenness of the French nation as a whole is academic. There will probably be as many opinions as people discussing the subject, for the whole situation remains confused, and the full facts of what happened have not yet come to light. Only the future will show what was the truth. But it can be shown, I consider, that those who led France in her hour of trial bear nine-tenths of the responsibility. The people did not realize in time that these men were not fit to lead them to victory. The Government kept on repeating that they would hold out to the last. "Paris," they said, "is in a state of defence," and a few days later they declared it an open town. "We will fight from North Africa if necessary," they proclaimed, and a short time afterwards they asked for the German terms. "We will not," they said, "accept a dishonourable Armistice," and they gave Hitler a blank cheque. They were not only unfit to lead, but they deceived the people. It is the prosecutors at the Riom trial who should be in the dock.

CHAPTER XIII

CENSORSHIP

THE rigidness of the French censorship showed a lack of trust in the intelligence and sangfroid of the people, which contributed to the confusion. Well-known and responsible journalists were not allowed to make any general comment on the war, though an occasional article slipped through the censor. Criticism of the censorship was so general that there was eventually a full-dress debate in the Chamber of Deputies, at which Blum made an excellent speech, castigating the officials of the Continental Hotel, where the French Ministry of Information was installed. Every time a visitor went into the hotel he had to fill up a form. It was as closely guarded as the War Office in Whitehall ; its function was to suppress information. There was the same mentality of defence rather than offence. The censors thought it better to delete, than to let anything pass of which they were at all doubtful, and they spent their harassed lives in a state of perpetual doubt. Hardly any of them were prepared to take any responsibility. It was thought better to stop journalists from making any comment in case some critical remark might incur the wrath of the Army Chiefs. It was thought better

to keep war correspondents away from the front in
case they should see something that they ought not to
see. There was a Maginot Line of hush-hush which
was deadening to the spirit. Just as the General Staff
had not had the confidence to attack the Siegfried Line
when Germany was engaged with Poland, so they had
not had the confidence to allow the Press to think for
itself and to speak for itself. With Parliament in recess,
there was all the more need to allow the Press to be a
vehicle of information both for the Government and
for the people. The Government had at its disposal a
means of helping the public to find itself during these
weeks of trial, but French journalism, as an independent
means of expression, was killed during those nine
months of warfare. There were officials at the Ministry
of Information who were doing their utmost to get
rid of the dead hand of bureaucracy, which had the
Ministry in its clutch, and who were trying to over-
come the excessive caution of the Military. Propaganda
ceases to be effective when the publication of official
communiqués or carefully controlled articles written
round those communiqués are the only war news
allowed. An intelligent public demands something
more than meagre official information served up with
enthusiastic accounts of the French Armies. Anything
optimistic was nearly always passed by the Censor,
and the optimistic method of writing was therefore
adopted by most French journalists and a few British.
One Paris correspondent of a well-known London daily
newspaper regularly sent out glowing accounts which

were given considerable prominence in the newspaper. For weeks the French public existed in a fool's paradise, continuing to live their normal lives, oblivious of a possible disaster. Every now and again their illusions would be temporarily shattered by Paul Reynaud, who made some magnificent speeches. The Prime Minister's rôle has always been that of a lone prophet, and he was crying out in a wilderness of official optimism which concealed an abyss of pessimism.

The case of the war correspondents was a glaring example of mis-spent opportunities for doing propaganda. They were unpopular with the French General Staff from the first. General Gamelin, when war broke out in September, stated that he did not want to have any journalists at the front, nor any broadcasts about the war. The General Staff wanted to keep the war to themselves, to be a military élite controlling the destinies of the country. They refused to admit that this was a new type of warfare in which the part played by the civilian could be almost as important as the part played by the soldier. They failed to realize that the very fact that Hitler knew little of military strategy, and that most of his generals had not served in the last war, was a strength, not a weakness. The German Staff broke free of military theory, which clouded French vision, and invented ingenious methods of breaking down the morale of the civilian population, which played as important a part in the achievement of success as the military operations themselves. Propaganda was used in every form by the Germans, but the

French would not even make use of their first-line troops—the war correspondents.

Reserve officers who had served in the last war should have been detailed off to look after the war correspondents. They should have had the authority to take them into the front line and to have remained with them there. As it was, journalists were handed over to Press officers belonging to the various armies, who had other jobs to do as soon as the real fighting began. War correspondents in modern warfare should be regarded almost as part of the army, as are Italian and German journalists, but at the same time they should have a free hand to write what they see, provided no important information is given the enemy. If the French, British and American publics could have received first-hand reports by well-trained journalists of what was happening at the front, they could have been made to realize that it was either *la lutte à l'outrance* or abject defeat. In the fight between ill-equipped French forces on one side, and well-organized mechanized columns on the other, there were many examples of fine heroism, which would have made stirring reading. To-day, as a result of the lack of such eye-witness stories, it is difficult to convince many that the French fought gallantly in many sectors.

War correspondents were not allowed to say very much even of what they did see. In May they witnessed the confusion caused by the refugees and guessed what the result might be ; they were in trains that were bombed ; they were nearly lynched by hostile crowds and they saw whole villages abandoning their houses after heavy bombings.   But they were not allowed to say that the refugees were blocking the roads and interfering with the movements of troops ; that they were spreading panic which disorganized local administration. There was an order that no mention must be made of the fact that trains and railways had been bombed, so that no warning could be given to civilians that it was safer to stay where they were than to try to move about. They were not allowed to say that at certain periods only military trains were allowed to run, and that it was useless for civilians to crowd the stations and so interfere with the entrainment of troops.   The newspapers could not start a campaign urging the Government to work out a policy with regard to the refugees, nor were they allowed to stir up the public to demand firmer action in general.   If American correspondents had been able to stay at the front, they could have helped to open American eyes to the seriousness of the situation before it was too late.   Britain, too, could have been made to realize how essential it was for a new expeditionary force to be sent immediately after the evacuation of Dunkirk.   The B.E.F. had only consisted of eleven divisions, and the French found it hard to understand why it was not possible for more well-equipped troops to be immediately sent to France.

Officials at the Continental Hotel complicated their own tasks by allowing far too many newspapers from all over the world to have war correspondents.   It was difficult to control them all and to know what to do with them.   The simplest way out was to make them

stay in Paris, whenever there was severe fighting.
Throughout the Continental Hotel there was a lack of
system, often characteristic of big offices run by retired
officers and journalists. There was a tendency for the
women assistants, many of whom had had business
training, to take control. This was the case in the office
dealing with war correspondents, nominally controlled
by a Colonel with a shade over one eye, who was the
stage type of the Deuxième Bureau, but it was his woman
assistant, " the little Napoleon " as we called her, who
was in charge. In the head censor's office it was the
sister-in-law of the Director who ruled. She started
the fashion of wearing imitation scissors in her hat.

At one period the censors were not content with the
blue pencil, but cut out any sentences or paragraphs
which offended them. Despatches were returned to
correspondents looking like a child's attempt to cut out
a paper pattern. There were so many stray pieces that
the fretwork had to be stuck on to another piece of paper
before it could be telegraphed or telephoned abroad.
In an article in which I described a night I had spent in
a French outpost on the banks of the Rhine, I said that
the Maginot Line " gave the impression of being almost
impregnable " ; the word " almost " was cut out. In
another despatch I had described the effects of air raids
on several towns, pointing out how little material damage
was done, and that the death-roll was comparatively
low ; I added an account of the bombing of a train,
which had caused only the deaths of a few chickens and
the wounding of a rabbit. The reference to the train

was censored, so that it appeared that as a result of the
bombing of several towns the only casualties had been
a few chickens and the wounding of a rabbit ! Unfortunately I could not stop the message going to London,
because at that time the telephone staff at the Continental
Hotel themselves telephoned all messages abroad direct,
as soon as they had been censored. London newspapers
often received copy which was quite incomprehensible,
but for several months they were not allowed to telephone to their Paris offices for explanations, nor were
the Paris offices allowed to telephone to their London
offices. Soon after this ban was lifted the Germans
bombed Amiens and Dieppe, and all telephonic communication between Paris and London was cut off,
anyway. Nearly all the despatches were sent to London
by cable via New York. If and when a correspondent
had the good fortune to see or hear something of a battle
and rushed back in his car to Paris to send his despatch,
it was often two days before it could be passed by the
military censor. On the other hand, news about the
same battle was being given out every day by Colonel
Thomas to the Paris journalists, and could be cabled
straightaway by them through the civil censors. Towards the end of May the military censorship was
speeded up, but until that happened the world's press
was dependent for its war news, not on the war correspondents, but on the Paris correspondents, who sat at
the feet of Colonel Thomas and were not allowed to
enter any of the military areas. This meant also that
one man, Colonel Thomas, was the source for all war

news published throughout the world, war correspondents having to content themselves with stories of a more general nature, which did not suffer from being delayed.

In those days there was often more to be learnt by finding out what news the Government was suppressing than what news they were allowing to be published. General Sikorski, for example, made a reference in one of his speeches to the restoration of Poland after victory had been achieved, but the passage never appeared in print because the Government had given orders that it should be cut out.

There was, however, one means of propaganda which the authorities did not control sufficiently well. When the Germans were only within about thirty miles of Paris, I went with Eddie Ward to broadcast my night bombing expedition over the German lines, which the B.B.C. wanted to have. No one asked to see my papers as I went into the building, and no one wanted to see what I was going to read at the microphone. After the expert had done his "This is Eddie Ward speaking," leaning in a 1900 attitude against the grand piano, I went and said what I had to say. I was told afterwards that no one had listened in to cut me off if I had said anything seditious. A fifth columnist could easily have seized the microphone to announce that the Germans had already surrounded Paris and that the city was about to be taken. It would have been a good opportunity, too, for a revolutionary leader to make his appeal to the people to defend their capital.

Paris and France needed stories which would stir their

national pride, and they could have been given by the Press. Instead the public was fed on uninspiring official communiqués and, later, on panic-making refugee tales. The result was that they went on leading their normal lives in Paris and elsewhere as if nothing unusual were happening. Each time I came back to Paris I was always struck to see the café crowds, the well-dressed women and the elegant young men thronging the Champs Élysées in the summer evenings as they had always done. Paris gave one an impression of *insouciance* that London does not give. French soldiers who saw Paris at play went back to the front with a bad impression. They did not see why they should sacrifice their lives when the people behind the lines were enjoying themselves. It was not long before the boulevards resounded to the tread of German soldiers and those same well-dressed women were weeping behind closed shutters or fleeing southwards from one village to another before the advancing enemy.

CHAPTER XIV

THE RETREAT FROM PARIS

THE fact that life went on normally in the heart of Paris made those last few days very tragic. I had seen villages and towns changed in a few minutes from crowded, busy life to confusion and emptiness, as the bombers passed over or the Germans approached. No one seemed able to bring themselves to believe that Paris's turn had come. By Monday, June 10, the Government had gone to Tours and the Germans were only twenty miles to the north of Paris ; on either side they were making a pincer movement. Where there should have been tremendous defensive activity, there was listlessness. Paris was still theoretically supposed to be in a state of defence. Whenever French sentries saw by my papers that I was a journalist, they wanted to know what was happening. I knew no more than they, only that the French forces were in retreat. Always they repeated : " Je ne comprends plus." No one understood, because they had not been allowed to understand. The sudden accumulation of bad news towards the end, which culminated in the capture of Paris, had a similar effect on the citizens as dive-bombing had had a month before on the soldiers. By keeping the public in ignorance the French Government had helped the Germans to carry out one of their chief tactics, the introduction of the surprise element.

Why was there no patriotic revolution ?   The answer is, I think, that the bourgeoisie were bewildered and still trusted the Government ; many of the leaders of the political Left were in prison as communists, or in exile ; the Fascist Right believed that it was on the way to obtain what it wanted through a German victory, and those among the soldiers who might have wanted to organize a revolt were not given the time to do so. Langeron remained at his post in charge of the Police, who had been armed some weeks before, and who were told to keep a look-out for any attempt to organize the defence of Paris.   While the centre of Paris was orderly and calm, the roads leading out of the capital were crowded by refugees, moving in serried ranks, sometimes no more than a few hundred yards an hour.   Outside the stations the roads were blocked for many hundreds of yards by people trying to take trains that often did not exist.   They used to wait, sometimes a whole day, sometimes a whole night, only to be told when they reached the ticket office that no trains were running. The British Embassy had left and the British Consulate was leaving, but no instructions were given to British subjects as to what they were to do.

On the whole the Parisians remained remarkably calm, although a surprise attack by air or land might have come at any moment.   Early on Monday morning I happened to motor through the Champs-Élysées, the Avenue des Grandes Armées and Avenue Foch ; every fifty yards a motor-bus was put slant-wise across the avenues with the object of stopping German troop-carrying 'planes from landing. The French secret service had learnt that such a surprise attack had been planned by the Germans. During the day the buses were removed, but the following night obstacles, such as dust-carts, were again put across the avenues. I have wondered what happened to those buses. There must have been at least 500 of them and each had two large tins of petrol, chained down inside. They would have been extremely useful for the evacuation of Paris, but I never saw any of them on the roads. That same evening there was a peculiar smell of smoke in the air and when we woke up in the morning it was impossible to see more than a few hundred yards out of the window. It seemed as if fires must have been started all round Paris by incendiary bombs. I went outside to find that every street was heavy with smoke and that it was impossible to see across the Place de la Concorde, nor from one bridge to another on the Seine. Everywhere there was silence, and Paris seemed to me to be a doomed city. I could not think of any explanation of the smoke except that Paris was burning; perhaps in a few days' time, I thought, one of the most beautiful towns in Europe would be razed to the ground with only the chimneys standing, like gravestones, to show where houses once had been. Fortunately there was an anti-climax to my dismal thoughts, for by eleven in the morning the wind had risen, the smoke had cleared and the sun was shining. There were many theories as to what had caused the

smoke pall ; one was that it had been put up by the
French authorities to enable trains to leave without being
bombed, and to protect the refugees on the road. As
the authorities were not making any attempt to help
civilians leave Paris, and had stopped nearly all the trains,
this seemed extremely unlikely. The more probable
explanation was that the wind had carried the smoke
from the burning oil tanks near Rouen and from German
smoke barrages over the Seine. Half of the Reuter
office had moved already to Tours some time before the
Government had left and were covering news to London
from there. It seemed time for us to get ready to move
the rest of our things from the Reuter office in the Havas
building, which was almost deserted, as the staff had
moved to Tours to be near the Government. There
were three of us left, Harold King, Courtenay Young
and myself, and we spent the morning burning all the
Reuter files in case there should be anything in them
which might interest the Germans. We then had
luncheon at Maxim's, the last meal they gave in unoccu-
pied Paris. We were joined by Sefton Delmer of *The
Daily Express*, Bob Cooper of *The Times*, Marriott and
Eddie Ward of the B.B.C. The restaurant was almost
deserted but the service was normal. As we left, and
the doors closed behind us, two wounded stragglers from
the Seine Battle came limping along the pavement.
Nearly all the shops and restaurants were closed and the
streets were deserted. At any moment, we felt, German
tanks might turn the corner of the Rue Royale. There
was no way of telling what point the invaders had

reached. We decided that we had stayed long enough and that we would move the next day.

Although most of the shops had shut and the owners had left, there were still a few doing business. My dairy and grocer were open, and I laid in provisions of food and cognac for the journey to Tours, which, judging by what we had seen of the state of the roads, might take us some days. The Scottish tailor, who had delivered me a pair of trousers the day before, was remaining, as he said he had no car, and he could not be bothered to wait in the queues at the station. By Tuesday it was only possible to leave from the Gare de Lyon, as all the other stations had been closed. I understand that the British public had no realization that Paris was about to be taken, and certainly English people and others coming up from the south of France had no idea. A party of English people arrived in Paris on the Tuesday from Italy. They went to the station, and after waiting hours in the queue were told that they could not have any tickets, as they had not got identity cards. They then found that it was quite easy to walk into the station without a ticket. They travelled for the next four days across France to Bordeaux without ever buying a ticket. Some of the adventures that people had getting out of Paris were extraordinary. A friend of mine who was on good terms with one of the station officials was smuggled into the Gare de Lyon dressed as a porter—the first of a series of amazing adventures.

On Wednesday morning, June 12, the day before the Germans bivouacked in the Bois de Boulogne on the

outskirts of Paris, we left in two cars, Harold King and
myself in one, Courtenay Young and Marriott in the
other.   Behind the two-seater Ford we had packed two
office typewriters, office files, luggage and a collapsible
canoe which I thought might be useful in enabling us
to choose our own time for leaving France, if the German
advance was not held up.   Unfortunately I left an
essential part of it in Paris and it was useless to us !   We
tried to leave due south from Paris by the Porte d'Orleans,
but were stopped by the police, as a new class of young
men had been called up and had been ordered to assemble
there.   It seemed unlikely that they were being mobilized
at this eleventh hour to fight on the Loire.   The authorities probably wished to have them under their control,
as they would be the most likely group of citizens, the
young student class, to try to organize the defence of
Paris.   It took us about three hours to cover the first five
miles out of Paris.   Sometimes we progressed only about
a hundred yards in the hour ; at other times at the rate
of two or three m.p.h.   We were in a serried column
of vehicles, three and sometimes four abreast, covering
every yard of the whole road ; some even tried to drive
along the sides, in and out of the trees.   At 6 o'clock in
the morning there was nearly a mile of cars in front of
us, and behind us lay another two miles of cars, whose
numbers were increasing from moment to moment.
A similar exodus had been going on for days from the
capital.   First the wealthy and now the shop-keeper and
poorer classes.   The majority of the cars had lain idle in
garages for many years and had been salvaged for the

retreat.   About six out of every ten had no self-starter, so that the occupants had to be very active.   We would be held up for, say, ten minutes at a time, and engines would be stopped for fear of using up petrol ; then came the signal that we were moving on, and out jumped the men and women with their starting-handles, feverishly cranking their engines ; if they failed to start there were shouts from behind and the occupants would have to push their recalcitrant and heavily loaded cars.   We would stop again after another ten or twenty yards, and so this tragi-comedy was repeated for hours on end, but everyone remained surprisingly cheerful.   After about five miles we managed to turn away from the column, which continued towards Rambouillet and was heavily bombed and machine-gunned later in the day.   When we managed to break free of the crowds along the attractive, wooded side-roads, everything was calm and peaceful in the hot sun, but once involved in a town or village, we realized how near we were to the war.

One of the many pathetic sights was to see the queues waiting to get petrol ; every now and again there would be violent quarrels, as someone tried to push up without waiting his turn.   In some of the towns we saw British N.C.O.'s on point duty, and the French military were in control at every big cross-roads.   We took nearly twelve hours to cover the seventy-five miles from Paris to Orleans, where we spent the night in our cars in the main square with hundreds of other refugees.   Marriott just managed to catch a British 'plane from the Orleans aerodrome, which got him to England that same evening. We reached Tours at luncheon time the following day.

CHAPTER XV

REYNAUD AND THE PEACE PARTY

PAUL REYNAUD has played a rôle in French politics rather similar to that played by Winston Churchill in British politics. His gloomy prophecies were disconcertingly accurate. He is able, courageous and possessed of the fighting spirit, which was so lacking in some politicians, but, unlike Churchill, he failed to carry the Government with him. Reynaud was not a ruthless leader, like Clemenceau ; he tended to compromise. When it was clear that France was not going to honour her engagements to her ally, Czechoslovakia, Reynaud, Campinchi and Mandel were on the point of resigning from the Government, but they were won over by that meretricious argument of not letting the Government appear divided at a critical moment in the country's history. Small, of poor physique, and no orator, though his speeches read well, he was not a leader to appeal to the French imagination ; many could not forgive him for having increased taxes as Minister of Finance. Because he himself had no popular or parliamentary backing he had to include others in his Cabinet who succeeded where he failed. He included men who were his critics, men of the political Right, who were in touch with the peace party. He thought he could absorb

them, but in the end they threw him out. The greatest
mistake he made was to nominate eighty-four-year-old
Marshal Pétain as vice-Premier, when he modified his
Cabinet on June 7. Pétain, the victor of Verdun, who
had proclaimed not in vain : " They shall not pass," was
a popular appointment. But those who knew him per-
sonally were apprehensive. Pétain had always been a
pessimist, age had made him a defeatist and vanity had
made him listen to German flattery, and feel a sympathy
for the German Army leaders. Hitler found in Pétain
another Hindenburg, on whose weaknesses he could play.
When the Marshal visited Cracow in May, 1935, to
attend the funeral of Pilsudski, Goering and officers of
the German Army went out of their way to flatter the
old man. The same policy was adopted when prominent Nazis and Staff officers met him at the funeral of
King Alexander of Yugoslavia, where he again repre-
sented the French Government. Daladier made a
mistake in sending Pétain as Ambassador to Spain, for
there it was easy for Germans and Italians to win him
over with fair words. Pétain had always felt that the
military class was an élite by itself, and he admired the
discipline of young Germany, Italy and Spain. When
he saw his country being laid prostrate before the
German advance, he believed that an honourable
arrangement could be reached between himself and
Weygand on one side, and the German Army leaders
on the other. He was either too stupid or too blind
to realize that France was not fighting the old type of
German Army, but Hitler and his satellites, who wanted

to enslave France body and soul. Even if he had ever read *Mein Kampf*, he was probably too honest and simple a man to realize that Hitler really meant what he had said. Seventy-three-year-old Weygand held rather similar views, though he was probably not deceived about Hitler's real intentions concerning France. Weygand was not pleased at taking over from Gamelin, when, as he believed, the war was already almost as good as lost. He did his best as Commander-in-Chief of the Allied Armies, but all the time he felt at the back of his mind, or so I believe, that France needed to suffer—that through defeat she would be purged of her sins, and, as a devout Roman Catholic, he felt very strongly about her sins. The idea that France might be purged through a *lutte à outrance*—through a magnificent fight to the bitter end which would call up all the best in the national character—did not appeal to him. It would have meant a long war and the possibility of a national uprising. He and Pétain had seen what had happened in Spain, and they preferred that the German High Command should take control rather than the French populace. Weygand has for a long time had leanings towards Fascism, and once or twice addressed meetings of Colonel de la Roque's Croix de Feu.

It was sufficiently dangerous that such views should have been held by the Allied Commander-in-Chief and the vice-Premier, but behind them was a peace party, which had been working in the country long before Munich. Whenever strong action was called for, the peace party had always stepped in to argue in favour of caution, and the Government had nearly always fallen into the temptation of taking the line of least resistance. Even when the Bonnets, the Lavals and the Caillauxs were not actually in the Government, they were actively lobbying in the Chamber and the Senate. By September, when war was declared, the French nation had rallied and had forgotten its political differences. The French man-in-the-street had had enough of Hitlerian aggression and was fully prepared to put an end to it through war. The voice of the peace party was not then heard. But after eight months of " phoney " war, and after the series of defeats in May and June, the peace party began to make itself felt again. It was especially active round the Elysée Palace and succeeded in winning over President Lebrun. These isolationists had always considered that it was no good fighting Germany, because she was sure to win, and they had always been against a war with Italy. They believed there could be a Fascist-Latin Bloc, which would hold Hitler in check. With the likelihood of the defeat of France, ambitious, unscrupulous men like Laval wanted to be in at the kill, and congregated round the harassed Government at Tours and then at Bordeaux. The pro-German peace party in France was more influential and more deep-rooted than the pro-German peace party in England had been before the outbreak of war, because the question was more a part of internal politics, which aroused such bitter feelings. The very fact that the political Left had wanted to support the Spanish Republicans during the Spanish Civil War, that they had wanted to prevent

German influence spreading in Eastern Europe, and had demanded that France should honour her obligations to Czechoslovakia, meant that the Right in politics tended to gravitate willy-nilly towards the peace party, the party that wanted France to lead a quiet life on her own, whatever happened outside her boundaries. All the old political and ideological animosities were once more aroused. At the same time, the dividing line was not at all clear. There was an influential group among the socialists, led by Paul Faure, who were in favour of peace at any price, and there were strong Rightist patriots, like Louis Marin, who were in favour of fighting Germany to the bitter end. The Munich settlement divided the nation into two hostile camps. On one side a delirious crowd escorted Daladier in triumph from the aerodrome at le Bourget to the War Office when he returned from Munich, and on the other side were those who turned away with humiliation and hatred in their hearts. It was difficult to effect any reconciliation between the " Munichites " and the " non-Munichites." That is how it came to be possible for people to say during those last days at Bordeaux, " Better Hitler than Blum " ; " Better the German occupation than a popular revolution " ; or, as the Croix De Feu put it : " Better Hitler than Democracy." Throughout the Battle for France this dangerous body of opinion was daily growing. It was an ideological rather than a class division. It struck down vertically through society, including Lebrun, members of the General Staff, politicians, members of the bourgeoisie, the socialist pacifists and many of the

working classes, who, confused by Soviet propaganda
since the Soviet-German agreement, believed it was better
that Hitler should win than that a " plutocratic Government" should remain. France had rallied to fight
Hitler, but defeat had led to disintegration again, and,
at the eleventh hour, she became once more a nation
divided against herself, broken up into individualist
groups pulling different ways. This was well exploited
by German agents, by people who appeared to be
respectable members of society. It was this background
which made it so dangerous to have men like Pétain,
Baudouin and Prouvost in the Government. It was
Paul Baudouin who announced that France would fight
to the bitter end if the German terms proved to be dishonourable, and then accepted those terms. It is doubtful whether he ever intended to let France fight, whatever the terms. It was Baudouin who stated, as Foreign
Minister, that it was only because of pressure from
England that France had stood in the way of Germany
having a free hand in Central and Eastern Europe ; he
even suggested that it was thanks to England that difficulties had been made about Germany taking Czechoslovakia. Baudouin, who had been little known until
he became Foreign Minister, wielded considerable power
in the Cabinet during the " capitulation" period. He
had been a Director of the Bank of France, Director-
General of the Bank of Indo-China and Director of a
Franco-Italian salt trust. This last had given him the
excuse to pay frequent visits to Italy, where he went as
a Laval agent to find out what possibilities there were of

coming to an understanding. Reynaud brought him into the Cabinet and was very dependent on him. Reynaud resigned but Baudouin remained, and Pétain in his turn found himself dependent. Another bad choice made by Reynaud was that of Jean Prouvost, Managing Director of *Paris Soir*, which had for long carried on a policy which, though not actually pro-German, was definitely not anti-German. He was backed by the industrialists of the north, the French Thyssens and von Krupps, who hated any form of Left Government and were prepared to back France's new Fascist state, even though it meant German occupation of their country. The appointment of the Croix De Feu Basque, Ybarnegaray, was the most surprising of all ; it was as if Oswald Mosley had been taken into the British Cabinet. He was the agent who started the conversations through the Spanish Ambassador, Lequerica, that led to the capitulation. These, and others, were the half-Quislings who prepared France's downfall. As " Sagittarius " wrote in the *New Statesman* :

> The French who did not wish to fight
> Were the ultra Left and the Fascist Right ;
> The victor managed a *coup de main*
> And France is hoist on her own Pétain.

There was, however, one stumbling-block to the peace party's plans. The Government, with Reynaud as their representative, had signed at a meeting of the Supreme War Council in London, a pledge that there would be no separate peace. After the bitter things that had been said in France about the Belgian betrayal, it was difficult for the peace party to do the same thing without manufacturing some excuse. The fact that Hitler had succeeded in forcing the B.E.F. to re-embark at Dunkirk, gave the peace party the opportunity to say that France had been abandoned by her ally at a vital moment of the battle. It was true that she had to face Germany almost single-handed in the Battle for France, aided only by small but gallant forces of British, Polish and Czech troops ; but the French knew that the British had prepared a new Expeditionary Force, which was on its way at the very moment that Paris fell. There was little attempt to fight a stiff rearguard action, so that the British should have time to arrive, and other French reinforcements be brought up from the south and east. British detachments found no difficulty in holding the line of the Seine defences against the Germans, but eventually they always had to retreat, because their flanks were exposed, the French having had orders to retire long before it was necessary. After the break through on the Somme and the Aisne, I do not believe that the French High Command made any serious attempt to hold up the Germans on the Seine or on the Loire. They and the peace party in the Government had abandoned the struggle, and had decided that it was no use defending Paris or waiting until the new B.E.F. arrived. It was easy then to arouse old animosities about perfidious Albion, who left her allies in the lurch. The French as a nation are probably as isolationist as the English. They do not like foreigners, though they are prepared on occasions to admire some of the British characteristics. Pétain himself felt after the 1914–18 war that England had not done all that she might have done, and that the brunt of the fighting had fallen on the French. He returned to the same charge about the 1940 war in a broadcast at the end of last June to justify capitulation. From that it was an easy step to argue that France was no longer bound by her pledge to England. Reynaud saw how the situation was developing and made a final attempt to rally the Government behind him. In the middle of June he made a last despairing appeal to the United States for immediate aid. If he had been able to obtain it, he could have silenced the critics in his Government ; but America could not, at such short notice, do more than she had already done. With that appeal Reynaud had played his last hand, and he, too, abandoned hope.

The persistent German propaganda for the last few years to separate Britain and France had appeared extra-ordinarily clumsy. It was so much in the interests of both countries to keep together that it had seemed impossible for such propaganda to succeed. But the Nazis persisted because they knew that there was fertile soil ready to receive it. They had taken note of that notorious article by Henri Béraud, quoted recently in an article by Alexander Werth. " I hate England in my own name and in the name of my ancestors," wrote Béraud in *Gringoire* in 1935. " I hate her by instinct and tradition. I say, and I repeat, that England must be reduced to slavery. . . . The day will come when the

world will have the strength and the wisdom to enslave
the tyrant with his reputation for invincibility. Con-
cord among the Continental nations alone can save
Europe and the world. Who knows ? Perhaps the day
is near." There were other weekly and daily newspapers which also carried on an undercurrent of anti-
British propaganda, such as *Candide*, *Je Suis Partout*, *Le
Jour*, *Action Française*, and, on occasions, *Le Matin*.

The Germans probably realized that no result would
have been achieved if France and England had had some
success, but they made a shrewd guess that it would be
otherwise if there should be a series of defeats, and they
were counting on these defeats. It was, therefore,
especially important that the French morale should have
been kept up by a series of attacks, immediately after the
declaration of war and throughout those eight months,
when the Germans did not take the initiative. Many,
who had long wanted firm action with regard to Germany, Italy and Japan, made the mistake of thinking that
once Britain and France had taken the plunge and had
declared war, everything would change and the Allies
would take aggressive action. But the old mentality
was too deep-rooted. Britain cannot be absolved from
blame. Even though it may be true that she sent to
France the quota of troops, for which the General Staff
had asked, namely eleven divisions, she should have
realized that the French were deceived about the impregnability of their defence line, and that they would
need more British troops when the big attack came.
The British Government must have known that the

French had not, as they said they had, mobilized as many as 5,000,000 men. Large numbers, also, were sent back after mobilization to work in the fields and the factories. Britain, too, was over-optimistic about her armaments production, using that facile slogan : " Time is on our side." We justified our inaction in the military field by arguing that, if we could play for time during those pre-war months, and during the " phoney " war period, all would be well. But Hitler's answer was the re-embarkation of the B.E.F. and the defeat of France.

The failure of the French High Command to order the withdrawal of the Allied Forces from Belgium immediately after the break through on the Meuse, had meant that the Allies were twenty-five divisions the less when it came to the Battle of France. Those divisions, as Mr. Churchill has stated, might have turned the scale. The Germans had lost heavily and were exhausted after their rapid advance ; there might have been a repetition of 1918, when the Germans, in spite of successive victories, suddenly collapsed in face of the Allies' stern resistance.

CHAPTER XVI

LAST DAYS AT TOURS AND BORDEAUX

TO come from the quiet villages of the lovely country-side into the crowded confusion of Tours was like entering the gateway with the inscription : "Abandon hope all ye who enter here." Senators, Deputies, politicians and Higher Military Staff had all abandoned hope, judging by the conversations that were heard. The censorship was suddenly lifted during those days in the middle of June, and for once we found it possible to describe the situation as we saw it. I sent a story suggesting that France was threatened with a defeat similar to that of 1870 ; the next morning Harold King sent an even more depressing story to Reuter, and no word was cut out in either. When these despatches reached London the censors were so surprised that they held them up for a considerable time, while they found out from higher authorities whether it was really true that France was in such a bad way ! Major Vautrin, an active soldier and a believer in Reynaud's policy, summoned the Press on June 13. What he had to say was intended as a pendant to Reynaud's appeal to the United States, which had been published that morning. Vautrin gave us a plain, unvarnished story of the situation on the Seine front, which could mean nothing else than serious defeat. He said that many French units had been in the front line for ten days without respite, whereas the Germans were repeatedly receiving reinforcements, and that the French were outnumbered by three to one. The Germans were attacking on the Seine front with 120 divisions at the maximum, which meant about 2,000,000 men, taking the German wartime division at 17,000. On the basis of Vautrin's calculations, France had only about 700,000 men, that is a third of the German forces. According to British officers, who were present on the Seine front, the French could have held the line with the numbers they had for several days longer than they did. There were many units of French artillery and French infantry who wanted to fight but were at a loss to know what to do because they had lost contact with other units, or because they had no officers to command them. The French Army had been trained to follow the old theory that you must always keep in front of the enemy, and if you are outflanked you must retreat until you are face to face with his line once more. But this was a war in which the Germans, by means of their speedy mechanized units and parachute troops, exploited the outflanking movement the whole time. The only way to deal with this was for the French to fight as isolated units and hold their ground as long as possible, keeping in mind the fact that they were outflanking the enemy as effectively as the enemy were outflanking them. An attempt to follow this method was made on the Seine with the defence in depths, and many German units were cut off and mopped up. On the Seine in the region of Vernon, Les Andelys and Pont des Arches, where the Germans broke through, the southern bank of the river is high and easily defendable and British troops remained fighting long after the French had left. But the French High Command had decided that the battle was lost and the order was given to retreat. After four weeks of continuous retreat it is difficult for an army to maintain its morale. While there were cases where isolated French units continued to defend themselves gallantly, being supplied with ammunition by air, the army as a whole was in rout. Officers were seen riding their chargers back from the front with girls sitting behind them. Soldiers were trooping along the roads, having thrown away their arms. If the line could have held, the French should have been able to bring up reinforcements by night when the German Air Force was not active.

I asked Major Vautrin whether it was true that the British were not helping the French in this great battle. He replied :

" That is not true, the Allies are fighting side by side."

Vautrin, it must be added, was not a Pétainist. It was at this conference that the first official announcement was made that Paris had been declared an open town. There were reports that Mr. William Bullitt, the American Ambassador, had been asked to negotiate with the German High Command to arrange for the entry into

Paris to be bloodless. That same evening, Thursday,
the German troops bivouacked in the Bois de Boulogne.
From the accounts given they seem to have been fresh
troops brought up for the propaganda victory parade
through Paris on June 14. Himmler arrived soon
afterwards from Berlin by air with a list of all the
prominent Jews and others who were "wanted" by
the Gestapo. German officers installed themselves in
luxury in the homes of wealthy Jews and fashionable
restaurants were reopened for their benefit. Their
wives and families came from Germany and the big
stores were full of German women purchasing silk
underwear and lingerie, which had been unobtainable
finery in Germany.

During these days, Tours was being bombed fairly
frequently and the Government decided to move to
Bordeaux. As had been the case in Paris, it was again
impossible to find out where the Germans were. There
were reports that they had broken through on the
Aisne and were advancing rapidly south on two lines,
one to the east of Paris towards Troyes, Dijon and the
Swiss frontier, and the other to the west of Paris through
Chartres, towards Le Mans and Tours. Half the Reuter
office had already left with Martin Herlihy, the Chief
Correspondent, to establish themselves in Bordeaux,
and the Havas Agency were packing up, and dismissing
all those whom they could not fit into their cars and
lorries. Our party had been joined by Eddie Ward
and Virginia Cowles and on Saturday, June 15, we
decided to follow the Government's example and to

quit. I must confess that our journey to Bordeaux was extremely pleasant, for we escaped the columns of refugees. We spent one night in a field by a small stream and drank vouvray in the village café in the morning. Village life was proceeding as calmly and peacefully as it had done for hundreds of years. It was only from the café gossip that one could tell that there was a war on. Virginia Cowles generally has a line on the local inhabitant and what they think, so that we talked to everyone we could, and when Harold King and I missed the other car behind, we knew that they had stopped in the last village so that she could sound its pulse. Wherever we went in the villages, the pulse was very firm. They did not have any intention of moving, whatever happened, but it was always possible that the passage of refugees would eventually wear down their calm and that they, too, would be caught up in the general exodus. We had only the wireless to keep us in touch with the outside world and we heard that the French Government had met that day in Bordeaux, and were continuing the meeting the next day, Sunday, as they had not come to any decision. The wireless was depressing, for it made us feel that we must leave the open country and hurry on to Bordeaux in order to find out what was happening. Bordeaux was as depressing as we had expected it to be. All available rooms were crowded with people, the majority sleeping on the floors, and the public squares were massed with cars where those fortunate enough to own a car were sleeping ; other people had to be content with the pavement. There were already about 7,000,000 refugees south of the Loire, and in a few weeks there were to be 10,000,000 refugees, 1,200,000 demobilized soldiers and 1,200,000 French prisoners released by the Germans.

The Cabinet, we learnt, was still discussing the question whether France should capitulate, or carry on the fight from North Africa. There were ugly rumours that the peace party was gaining ground. The sinister Laval could be seen lobbying at cafés. Waverers were being won over by the argument that there was no harm in asking the Germans their terms, and that if the terms were dishonourable the struggle would be continued from North Africa. The "men of the capitulation" knew well enough that once the Government was caught up in negotiations with regard to terms, it would be very difficult to draw back, but the waverers fell into the trap. It was left to Mandel, a calm but tragic figure, to announce on Sunday night that those who were in favour of a fight to the bitter end, Reynaud, himself, Monnet, the Socialist, Louis Marin and others, had been defeated ; the Reynaud Government had fallen and Pétain was Prime Minister. That, we knew, meant the end of resistance ; the new Government would ask for the terms and would be forced to accept them, whatever they were. There would be no question of continuing the fight from North Africa. But even so, Paul Baudouin, who remained as Foreign Minister, continued the subterfuge of pretending that they still intended to fight if the terms were not satis-

factory.   Sir Ronald Campbell, the British Ambassador,
did his utmost in trying to persuade the new Government
to maintain their pledge to Britain that they would not
sign a separate peace, and in trying to persuade them to
continue the struggle from the colonies.   M. Zaleski,
the Polish Minister, and other diplomats also visited
members of the Government.   On Monday, June 17,
they were still being told by Baudouin that the Pétain
Government was a continuation of the Reynaud Government and intended to carry out the same policy of
resistance, if the terms were unsatisfactory.   He told
the mission, consisting of Lord Lloyd and Mr. Alexander,
who had been sent out by Mr. Churchill, that the
Government intended to leave the next day for Per-
pignan, whence they would proceed to North Africa.
If there were any members of the Government who
really had such an intention, they changed it when
Bordeaux was heavily bombed the same day.   But still
the peace party was not absolutely certain of their
ground.   Feeling was running high among officers and
numbers of the politicians who had learnt what was
happening, and it was decided to arrest Mandel, regarded
now as the leader of the " revolt."   Subsequently, as a
result of a strong protest made by Herriot and Jeanneney,
the Presidents of the Chamber and of the Senate, Mandel
was released and Pétain stated that it had all been a
mistake.   It is probable that the old man understood
very little of all the intrigues which were on foot in
Bordeaux to bring about the downfall of France.   He
still believed that Germany, the victor, would give

fair terms to an enemy defeated on the field of battle.

In the meantime there was the problem of getting British subjects out of France. There were big queues at the Consulates of all the western ports, Bordeaux, Nantes, St. Nazaire and St. Jean de Luz. British liners on the way home were told to stand by off various small harbours along the coast, where it was hoped they would not be discovered by German bombers. As the liners arrived the British were sent on board by tender, as were also a number of French people. From the point of view of journalism it was one's duty to remain in France and report how matters developed, as some correspondents did. But many of us felt that with the defeat of France an early attempt might be made to invade Great Britain, and that it was time to get back to do what one could to help to repel any such attempts. The British Embassy arranged for journalists on Monday, June 17, to embark on the S.S. *Madura*, which was lying off Le Verdon, north of Bordeaux. German bombers were searching for all boats lying off the coast embarking British troops and civilians. It was that same afternoon, to the north of where we lay, at St. Nazaire, that they sank the Cunard-White Star *Lancastria*, carrying 6,000 British troops, of whom nearly 4,000 were lost. A number of bombs fell near the S.S. *Madura*, but none hit us though the German wireless announced that we had been sunk, and on Tuesday we sailed away from the shores of defeated France. We left behind many British citizens who had the greatest difficulty getting away, and some were forced to remain. By the middle of the week there were no Consular representatives to arrange for their departure, although they should be, like captains of a ship, the last to leave.

Before we boarded the liner we had confirmation that the fight was ended ; Pétain had already made his " il faut cesser le combat" speech. While motoring to the harbour, we stopped to ask the way in a small village just as a woman rushed out of a house, beside herself with grief. She had heard Pétain's speech on the wireless. The girl who served us luncheon at the harbour was gay and charming until someone told her the news, when she burst into tears and served the rest of the meal, red-eyed and sobbing. There was no rejoicing that France had ceased to fight. There was no sign of anti-English feeling then among the people ; they realized that their only hope of ridding themselves of the Germans was through the British. But at a time of intense disillusionment it is easy to work on people's feelings, and we knew that the Government would develop their anti-English theme. We felt no surprise listening to Paul Baudouin's broadcast on board the boat that Monday evening when he stated : " The forty million Frenchmen found themselves before the Battle of France almost alone against the eighty million Germans to whom the menace of the Italian Army was added. . . . Insufficiently prepared for totalitarian warfare, our friends and Allies have not been able in time to give the help necessary to the advance guard constituted by the French Army. That is why our Government, presided over by Marshal Pétain, had to ask the enemy what his conditions would be." But the conclusion of the speech came as a shock. "France is not ready," he said, "and it will never be ready, to accept dishonourable terms, nor to abandon the spiritual liberties of our people and betray the soul of France. The French people can save the spiritual values to which they are attached more than to life itself, but if they are obliged to choose between existence and honour, their choice is made—and by their total sacrifice, it is the soul of France and all that it represents to the world that they will have saved."

This was deception on the big scale, on the Hitler–Goebbels scale. It was an attempt to dope the public by grandiloquent words, so that they would accept their betrayal. Pétain was more honest when he suggested in his broadcast that the sufferings of millions of refugees had influenced the Government to make its decision. Baudouin's bluff had already been called by the British offer of a Franco-British Union, according to which there was to have been common citizenship, a single war cabinet and the formal association of both parliaments. "The nations of the British Empire are already forming new armies," stated the British proposal. "France will keep her available forces in the field, on the sea and in the air. The Union will concentrate its whole energy against the power of the enemy, no matter where the battle may be. And thus we shall conquer." The French Government could have avoided further bloodshed for the moment by accepting defeat in France and retiring to North Africa to continue the struggle

from there.   The British Navy, with the French, would
have had the responsibility of escorting them, and those
troops who were to continue the fight.   Once in North
Africa they could have made their terms about effective
British participation in the war by land.   It would have
been a heroic decision, for it would have meant leaving
French citizens without protection, such as the Government thought it would be able to give them under a
régime of "relative independence."   But the situation
called for heroic decisions.

   From being close allies, Britain and France suddenly
found themselves almost at enmity with one another,
and it was not long before diplomatic relations were
broken off.   Hitler had achieved one of his ambitions.
To many of us aboard the ship, who had lived long in
France, this was as tragic as is the sudden enmity between
a brother and a sister, or between a husband and a wife.
In the tense atmosphere of that ship, where there were
1,600 extra passengers, quarrels broke out between the
anti-French and the pro-French, which was symptomatic
of what might be expected in many parts of the world
for some time to come.   But recriminations from either
side are void and meaningless.   France still needs us as
we need France, not because of any natural sympathy
between the nationals of the two countries, but because
it is important to preserve the civilization which we
share.   "If we open a quarrel between the past and the
present, we shall have lost the future," said Churchill
in the fine speech he made to the House of Commons
the day after the French Government had announced

that they had decided to end the struggle. There was no recrimination in his speech. After explaining why there had only been three British divisions left in France to fight the last battle, he praised the valour of the French Army. "If we are now called upon to endure what they have suffered," said the Prime Minister, "we shall emulate their courage, and, if in final victory rewards are ours, they shall share the gains—aye, freedom shall be restored to all. We abate nothing of our just demands: Czechs, Poles, Norwegians, Dutch, Belgians—all who have joined their causes to our own, all shall be restored. What General Weygand called 'The Battle of France' is over. I expect that the 'Battle of Britain' is about to begin. Upon this battle depends the survival of the Christian civilization. Upon it depends our own British life and the long-continued history of our institutions and our Empire. The whole fury and might of the enemy must soon be turned on us. Hitler knows that he will have to break us on this island or lose the war. If we can stand up to him all Europe may be free and the life of the world may move forward into broad and sunlit uplands. If we fall, then the whole world, including the United States, and all that we have known and cared for, will sink into the abyss of a new dark age made more sinister and perhaps more prolonged by the light of a perverted science. Let us therefore do our duty and so bear ourselves, that if the British Commonwealth and Empire lasts a thousand years, men will say, 'This was their finest hour.'"

CHAPTER XVII

THE LESSON OF FRANCE

THE lesson of France is that we cannot fight this war with old methods, that it is a mistake to think that time is on our side, and that we must keep up our fighting morale. The French kept on proclaiming how strong they were, but they were never quite certain that it was true, for they had been kept from testing their own strength in their own time. The *Corps francs*, the mobile French patrols, were a fine body of men with high confidence because they were constantly in touch with the enemy and knew that they were as good, if not better. Similar bodies of men could be formed now to make raids on the weakly defended German coast-line stretching from Narvik to the Pyrenees, and on the long Italian coast-line. Raiding parties which strike quickly and retire quickly can make an enemy very nervy, as instanced by the effect in France of the feeling that the Germans might be anywhere round the corner. Once there had been a few false telephone calls made and a few parachutists captured, the populace themselves carried on the confusion by spreading wild stories about the presence of the enemy. We must take a leaf out of the German notebook, for this is no " gentleman's war." We must dress in German uniforms, if necessary, and forget all that we have been taught about "playing the game."

The young German soldier and officer is fanatical; even when their lives could only be saved by blood transfusions in the French hospitals they would refuse foreign blood and prefer to die kissing Hitler's photograph; when advancing to battle they seemed sometimes to be on the verge of hysteria; they trained themselves to go without food and water and could march forty miles in the day. Fanaticism is excellent for attack, but it is less good when the enemy are carrying on a guerrilla warfare, and when there are reverses. It remains to be seen how the young German stands up to defeat.

As to the question of the invasion of England, it is clear that the lesson of France has been brought home to the Government. Orders have been given that the population must stay where they are in the event of an attack. The lesson of France to each individual is that, apart from helping the military by staying put, it is also the safer thing to do. Any attempted invasion will certainly be accompanied by heavy bombing, and probably by the dropping of parachutists and troops from troop-carriers, in which case no one place is safer than anywhere else.

"The lesson of this disaster must be learned by Great Britain," said General de Gaulle in an interview with George Slocombe in *The Sunday Express* recently. "If bombardments occur, if invasion comes, the people must not be allowed to encumber the roads. They must stay where they are." Asked for his own explanation of the defeat of a great army which the French nation and its Allies regarded as invincible, the General said : " It was the inevitable result of the shock of an encounter between an army organized on outworn principles and an army organized for modern mechanical warfare. The French Army had been created to fight on a stable front. When the front disappeared it found that it could not go on fighting. The army was dislocated from top to bottom, and actually there was greater confusion and disorder at the top than at the bottom. The High Command found itself no longer in control of the situation. It lost courage.

" That is one reason. Another, and of great importance, was the evacuation of great populations. The flight of these millions of refugees, the panic spread by their movement across the country, the rumours and confusion and breakdown in internal communications caused by their flight contributed largely towards the defeat."

With regard to the activities of the Fifth Column in France, General de Gaulle stated in the interview that enemy agents were able to influence the counsels of the highest to a considerable extent. Even Paul Reynaud was pushed to the verge of despair by their efforts among the members of his own immediate circle. Enemy agents were able to spread panic and defeatism among the Government, the Senate and the Chamber, and, above all, in the High Command.

Reynaud knew what a German victory would mean,

but he was unable to convince his entourage. In a speech at the beginning of June he said : " The risk which must be realized in Europe and outside Europe to-day is known to all the world. It is a régime of oppression where men who are not Germans are but slaves. The new world announced by Hitler in his proclamation may begin perhaps by trickery, but soon enough will follow orders for the bullying of the workers and the moral and physical destruction of the élite. It would be the Middle Ages again, but not illuminated by the mercy of Christ."

What he foretold is taking place in his country to-day. But hope rests with the French soldiers, sailors, airmen, and civilians in exile, led by General de Gaulle, with the French people themselves, whose individualism, though it contributed to their defeat, will help them to survive as a nation, and with the British Commonwealth of Nations which will not desist from the war until final victory is achieved. The Pétains and the Weygands may have succeeded for the time being in suffocating a national uprising, but the revolution will come when German power has been broken. That a clique of men should have succeeded in turning Britain's ally into what amounts almost to an enemy power is the tragedy of France. " Later, with the passing of time," recently wrote Elie J. Bois, for twenty-five years Editor of the *Petit Parisien*, " when, as I hope, this nightmare will be no more than a sad memory, the most astounding features will appear to be the sadistic act of these ' men of the capitulation ' in concealing it beneath the prestige of a Marshal of France who did not merit such treatment, and, further, the fantastic vanity with which they presented themselves as saviours, to a public opinion which was ignorant and deceived. They would even demand that Frenchmen should consider them, like Clemenceau, like Poincaré, like Joffre, like Foch, as national heroes, and that England should be thankful to them. The future—let us have faith in it—will correct all that, for the honour and happiness of our two peoples."

INDEX